THE
30
LAWS
of
FLOW

THE
30
LAWS
of
FLOW

Timeless Principles for
Entrepreneurial Success

Charlene Day

Address inquiries to the publisher:
Potentials Within
www.potentialswithin.com

Canadian Cataloging in Publication Data
The 30 Laws of Flow: Timeless Principles for Entrepreneurial Success
A 30 Day Plan to Magnify Your Flow of Time, Money & Productivity
ISBN 978-0-9695781-3-0

---

1. Universal Laws 2. Quantum Field Theory 3. Success 4. Entrepreneur 5. Goal (Psychology) 6. Spiritual Life 7. Success in Business 8. Thought and thinking 9. Self-Management (Psychology) 10. Meditation 11. Mind 12. Mindfulness 13. Change (Psychology) 14. Habits 15. Title

Services
Keynote Speaker
Business and Entrepreneur Coach
Individual and Group Mentoring

Cover Design by Patti Knoles
Text design and layout by Heidy Lawrance of WeMakeBooks.ca
Print Production by Beth Crane of WeMakeBooks.ca
Illustrations by Nuwanthi

Printed and bound in Canada

Table of Contents

Foreword

*I*t is not uncommon for an individual holding a holy Bible in their hands to refer to it as a book. However, the beautiful truth is that the Bible is a library of books…66 books in fact. Likewise, The 30 Laws of Flow, is a library of information pertaining to the Laws that govern your life.

The basic law of life is create or disintegrate…grow or die. As you bring your life into harmony with the laws of your being, you grow; you expand your awareness and your perception of life and all that is in it is broadened. Unfortunately, the masses of people live like minnows in the shallow. They never get out into the deep where real life is flowing.

What Charlene Day has prepared for us within the pages you have in your hand goes well beyond a book. You have a library of material pertaining to the laws of your being, the value of which extends well beyond the scope of your imagination.

I once read that no amount of reading or memorizing will make a person successful in life. It's the understanding and *application* of wise thoughts that count. Every page in this book is crowded with wise thoughts. Even half an effort to act on the material you're about to cover would have the ability to multiply your income greatly. The secret to whatever good you desire is locked up in the laws that govern your being and this book, *The 30 Laws of Flow*, explains them beautifully.

I fell in love with the title of this book when I first heard it. The word "Laws" and "Flow" belong together. You and I truly live in an ocean of motion. Spirit flows to and through us. It's important that we understand that the Law is God's modus operandi; it's how everything is done. The Spirit of God flows to and through everyone and everything, and we must understand that Spirit never expresses itself other than perfectly. The trick of life is to understand the Laws and then bring your life in harmony with them.

James Allen put it very well when he said, "You do not attract that which you want, but that which you are."

Make up your mind right now that you are not going to rush from page to page. Understand that it's not important that you even finish reading this book but it's vitally important to the success and fulfillment of your life that you do understand and apply what you read. You may read the same paragraph ten times. And realize, if you're having difficulty with it, it's because you're not in the flow.

Let Charlene Day's masterpiece help you create a beautiful flow from this point on in your life.

Bob Proctor,
Featured teacher in *The Secret*, bestselling author of *You Were Born Rich*

Preface

You may be wondering how the Laws of the Universe can be connected with entrepreneurial success. Well, you're not alone: it took me years to make the connection myself.

As an entrepreneur, personal development is essential and through years of innumerable courses, books, workshops, coaching, writing and teaching, I've been able to observe many successful entrepreneurs. Entrepreneurs bring change into the world. They make things different, and they make themselves different too in the process. They regenerate, revolutionize, transform, modify and look for solutions to create "better" lives.

But what struck me was that the successful ones all had certain characteristics in common, and the most powerful one was that they had developed habits that led them to be very accomplished.

For example, I saw them being single-minded around their "worthy ideal" or purpose and having an unshakable faith that their goal would be become a reality. I noticed they had developed a connection with the higher part of themselves that helped them cultivate and nurture this. They also were comfortable with discipline and able to develop habits such as utilizing their unique ability and delegating the rest, continuous learning, regular goal setting with set outcomes, focus, organization, planning, measuring results, consistency, team building, thinking win-win, keeping healthy and in balance, just to name a few of their success practices.

Discipline was a hard one for me to understand at first, because my childhood associations with the word were hard to overcome. But I've learned that the purpose of discipline is quite simple: it gives us the necessary *structure* to bring about changes that we desire. Adopting new habits is easier with discipline. Even more, when you self-design a program, it is all the more valuable because you are the architect. You can agree to set up a new habit and with discipline it is now non-negotiable. The discipline of quieting the mind may be one of the most impactful *structures* you adopt. This behavior can re-shape your life and your goals to lead you to your version of success.

But that wasn't all these special entrepreneurs had; there was something else. Something mysterious that I couldn't quite put my finger on for a long time. They seemed to be accessing some aspect of living that most people weren't.

Finally, it came to me: not only were they connecting with their higher self, they were using the *structure* of the Universal/Eternal/Cosmic Laws to create the results they wanted. They were open to access a higher level of consciousness that allowed them to manifest success. So why couldn't we ALL do that?

That's why I wrote this book. To do four things:

1. To introduce you to a powerful selection of Universal/Eternal/ Cosmic Laws, gathered and explained all in one place.
2. To extend an invitation to you to reconnect with the spiritual aspect of yourself (your highest self) in whatever form is comfortable to you so that you can access your greatest wisdom and translate it into your personal and business life.
3. To guide you on a journey to help you apply these Laws through developing new habits or rituals, replacing and interrupting old ones, to liberate you from your programmed responses.
4. To bring together quantum physics, understanding of our brain functioning and the Universal Laws to reinforce that you have access to infinite potential and can mold your reality through your thoughts (the most potent form of energy).

As Bob Proctor says, "It's the understanding and *application* of wise thoughts that count."

Once you become aware of the *structure* of the Universe and integrate some of the suggested applications for each Law, it will be easier to be connected with the Flow in all your creations, just like the most successful entrepreneurs you see today.

No longer are these secrets held by a special few. Now you hold them in your hands, and you can use them to do whatever you dream of doing.

Namaste,

Charlene Day

Acknowledgments

I am grateful to a very long list of teachers and mentors such as Barbara Marx Hubbard, Blair Singer, Bob Proctor, Brian Tracy, the late Brian Klemmer, Bruce Lipton, Christy Whitman, Dalai Lama, Dan Sullivan, David Suzuki, Deepak Chopra, Eckhart Tolle, Ester Hicks, Frances Moore Lappe, Greg Braden, Harv Eker, Helen Palmer, Jack Canfield, Jack Kornfield, Jean Houston, Joe Dispenza, Joel Barker, John Assaraf, Julia Butterfly Hill, Kathy Kolbe, Loral Langemeier, Louise Hay, Lynn McTaggart, Lynn Twist, Marianne Williamson, Mark Victor Hansen, Mary Morrissey, Maureen Jennings, Michael Beckwith, Neale Donald Walsch, Pema Chodron, Robert Allen, Robert Kiyosaki, Roger Barnett, Russ Hudson, Sandra Leask, Sandy Gallagher, Sharon Salzberg, Thich Nhat Hanh, Tony Robbins, the late Wangari Maathai and Wayne Dyer. All of these people touched me and through their sharing of wisdom have influenced the content of this book in immeasurable ways.

I am especially grateful for Bob Proctor demonstrating the importance of repetition. Thank you, I finally got it.

No one can succeed alone and I want to thank all who made this book and its programs a reality: Peggy McColl for her guidance as my book coach, my grammatical editors Jan Kreut and Gail Christison, Patti Knoles for a fabulous cover design, Lisa Cherney for her assistance with marketing copy and Rodney Ronquillo for the beautiful soothing piano as the background for some of the earlier meditations.

A very special thanks goes to my overall editor and writing coach, Kristelle Bach Sim. I totally loved our brainstorming sessions. Her research and inspired contributions lent a magical touch to this book.

I partner with many talented individuals and I am very grateful for their substantial insights during this writing process: my Mastermind members, my joint venture partners, and the 30 Day Plan beta group, who gave me great testimonials after participating in the first version of the 30 Day program. Thank you all.

I so appreciate all my friends who cheered me on this year and my Enneagram and Shaklee families who supported me.

My immediate family contributed to all of this, not only with household management but with understanding, giving me the time I needed to concentrate and focus. Thank you so much for allowing me to live my passion.

Most importantly, I am forever grateful for the unseen support and connection I feel everyday with the Infinite Universal Consciousness, the Universal Mind. This is ultimately where I receive my greatest strength. Thank you, thank you!

Blessings to you all!

Introduction

I have always been a seeker. A very curious soul. Constantly asking questions; trying to figure out life. Why are we here? What is the meaning of our existence? What did we come to do? How does it all work?

I used to drive my parents crazy with the kinds of questions I was asking. They didn't know the answers, so I began to read everything I could get my hands on in the areas of holistic health and wellness, commerce, personal development and spirituality. I started studying with teachers, trainers, guides, coaches, spiritual gurus and taking group programs.

Early in my journey, I completed a four-year program which gave me a Bachelor of Spiritual Science. This program was my first introduction to the ideas:

- That we are *spiritual* beings having a *human* experience.
- That thoughts are things or energy (very potent energy).
- That we create our reality either consciously or unconsciously through our own subconscious programming (includes our thoughts, feelings and words).
- That our body is our vehicle, our expression of our spirit.
- That as powerful creators, we collectively create our world.

That program also introduced me to the magnificent tool of meditation. Using guided meditations or meditative music or sitting in silence, I connected with other meditators in a shared energetic realm. I began to practice mindfulness, and made a conscious effort to put my full awareness into anything that I was doing. I started to notice the miracles of life, each moment. I learned about holistic healing. I became a vegetarian, feeling more connected to the earth by eating this way and feeling a lighter, higher vibration. This was where I was first introduced to the Laws of the Universe, and learning about them changed my life.

One of the first things I was taught was that the universe around us is a very orderly place in which nothing occurs by chance. From the spiritual to the physical to the mental, everything that happens does so according to Law, and each system has its own set of Laws. For instance, the natural world we see (known as the Newtonian world) operates based on Newtonian Laws: the entire universe is a giant machine, made up of mechanical parts called particles. It runs according to distinct mechanical Laws.

But recently, advanced physics has uncovered the powerful and mysterious Quantum world, and its behavior and qualities are described with Quantum principles: all reality springs from an invisible energy called the Field, and matter is a result of wave functions emanating from this Field. Although this is still a fairly new idea, even during Einstein's time he proclaimed, "The Field is the sole governing agency of the particle."

When we talk about Universal/Eternal/Cosmic Laws, we are focusing more on the Quantum side of things. The 30 Laws of Flow are all founded on the understanding that everything in the universe is energy, including us. The Laws are potentially predictable and repeatable, lending to an operational structure but are far more complex than simple Newtonian mechanics. However, with enough knowledge and awareness, we benefit from knowing how they work and using them to our advantage.

Now here's the important thing for us: whether we are aware of these Laws or not, they are still in operation. They won't change because we don't like them or agree with them. They are a constant framework. Even though we cannot see the Laws, or hear them, smell them or taste them, they are present. Like the Law of Gravity, they apply to everything and everyone.

Bob Proctor points out in a reprint of *The Science of Getting Rich* book, "You can act in accordance with these laws, or you can disregard them, but you can in no way alter them. The laws forever operate and hold you to strict accountability, and there is not the slightest allowance for ignorance. Once a person learns and obeys these laws, he will get rich with mathematical certainty."

When I first learned about the existence of these Laws, I was young and didn't fully get the implication of the power of these Laws in my life. In my entrepreneurial quest I began to study with Bob Proctor again and I was reminded of the great influence of these Laws in our lives. My awareness was piqued once again. I also listened to Mary Morrissey speak on the Laws from Raymond Halliwell's book. I studied Deepak Chopra's book on the Laws, as well.

I realized that once we become aware of the Laws of the Universe, we can also learn to apply them to our advantage. When we do that, we are able to achieve whatever it is that we want from life. I also noticed that when I honored these Laws, I felt like I was in the flow, in harmony with all that is. I am going to suggest, that when we connect with that flow of energy, we merge with The Divine as a co-creator. We connect to who we really are.

In 2012 there was quite a buzz around the Mayan calendar and the misinterpretation of the ending of that age as being the end of the world. It was the end of an era and since everything is energy, frequency, and in constant motion, it was the end of the *world's vibrational level* as we knew it. We are now in the Age of Aquarius and the time has finally come for us to wake up out of the trance we have been in. This new age of consciousness is bringing a new awareness, a new energy, and an awakening to the real field of all possibilities. More and more people are becoming mindful and waking up to the fact that we can consciously create a new reality because we are vibrational beings. We are at a crossroads where more people are accessing higher levels of consciousness. We are becoming more aware of ourselves, the nature of life, and the interconnectedness of all things. The last frontier is being explored - the mind. It really is an exciting time to be alive. We are experiencing a real shift. We have so much potential and are now learning how to develop it. More of us are becoming aware that we are spiritual beings and tapping into our divine connection. When we do that, we are in the flow.

I am so grateful for all the teachers who have mentored me over the years keeping me aware of all the possibilities. Every one of them gave me another piece of the puzzle to reach higher and higher levels of conscious awareness, and each piece has changed my life. Since we are the direct result of our thoughts and the people we hang out with and the books we read, I chose to immerse myself with these mentors and teachers. Being with them or their knowledge is a constant reminder to stay with the higher consciousness as it is so easy to be sucked back into current reality with our five senses on autopilot. We are living lives full of ingrained habits, emotional programming and cultural reinforcements that need to be challenged **daily**.

Finally, I realized that I had the responsibility of passing along this knowledge. It was time to step into my power. To stop playing small. So I started writing books myself. My earlier books were focused in the health and wellness arena and now I am branching out into my other passions, especially self-development and spirituality. This book is a labor of love and a gesture of gratitude to all my teachers, and a way to encapsulate everything I have learned with real stories of my own transformation. Even though I am not an expert when it comes to the Laws, I am still exploring and changing daily with each new revelation. I invite you to join me in this amazing journey.

What is Flow?

"All things are in motion and nothing is at rest...
You cannot go into the same (river) twice."
Heraclitus

*I*n the dictionary, flow as a verb "means to move along or move out steadily and continuously in a current or stream; to circulate; abounding; having in excess; proceeding smoothly or easily".

As you study the Laws of the Universe in this book, you will learn that everything is energy. We live in an ocean of motion. Everything in life is in a constant state of flux, it moves, vibrates and travels in circular motions. So we could say that everything is always flowing. When we are in harmony with the Laws of the Universe, we are reconnected to the flow. Currently, I believe there is a great yearning for this state of being.

In his book, *Money is Love: Some Things are Worth Believing In: Book 3* author Klaus Joehle said, "The universe is saying: Allow me to flow through you unrestricted and you will see the greatest magic you have ever seen." Flow with your breath in the present moment. Focus just on your breath. It is only when your engrained thoughts interfere with the flow in life that you get stuck between what we perceive as pain and pleasure.

In 1975 in the area of positive psychology, Mihaly Csikzentmihalyi in his book *Flow: The Psychology of Optimal Experience*, characterized flow as the complete absorption in what one does. He developed the concept of flow as an optimal experience: a mental state of operation in which a person performing an activity is fully immersed in a feeling of energized focus, full involvement, and enjoyment in the process of the activity.

In a flow state, we might experience a sense of serenity, in harmony with all that is, feeling that we are in the present moment, inspiration, a sense of ecstasy, joy, playfulness, being centered, or inner clarity. We could also be completely involved, singularly focused, experiencing complete concentration as Mihaly Csikzentmihalyi suggests.

Think back over your life and see if you can relate to this sense even if it was only for a brief time. I venture to say that most people will have experienced a sense of flow at some time or another. I also believe that many of us are looking for more flow in our lives–that sense of expansion, connection and inspiration, being in the present moment. Just take a breath and you will notice that once you inhale, you experience an exhale very naturally. This cycle of breathing is an example of flow in our lives.

Many people say they are looking for happiness but when you study the Laws, you will see the Law of Polarity shows us that in order to know happiness, we have to also know sadness. In our dualistic world, you can't know happiness without experiencing sadness. This goes for all of our emotional states. It is one of the privileges and greatest challenges of our human experience. We can choose to be happy as an adopted attitude but I propose that what we are looking for is more appropriately described as flow or harmony, serenity, joy, bliss or love. Flow seen in this way is an acceptance, a receptive state of being.

It is not your business to figure out flow, but it IS your business to get into it. When you don't understand and/or live in harmony with the Laws, you will experience suffering. Those Laws are not biased–they don't care if you know about them or not, they will operate no matter what. They are fixed and they operate despite one's ignorance (not knowing).

But when you think, act and feel in a certain way or shift your vibration into a new way of thinking and being, it puts you in harmony with the Universal/Eternal/Cosmic Laws. You then become a vibrational match to whatever you desire. You are in harmony with your own nature and the flow of the universe. You are in the natural stream of your own life force, feeling inspired and aligned with all the unforeseen things that come to support your desires.

While on the subject of desires, how about health and wealth? Health is a natural state of consciousness to which everyone has access. Wealth comes in our state of consciousness where we realize our value and give that value in service to others. Both subjects could have great volumes written on them, but ultimately people are looking for good health, prosperity, time freedom, peace of mind, spiritual connection, creative expression, a passionate career, and good long-lasting relationships.

Regardless of your desires in life, you have an innate ability to transform your current circumstances. You can do this by understanding and applying these Universal/Eternal/Cosmic Laws and changing your energetic vibration. Since everything is energy and flow represents movement, flow feels like the most appropriate way to describe a state of being in harmony with all the Laws of Universe.

My wish, as you study and apply these Laws to your life, is that you begin to experience more days of feeling in the flow, serenity, harmony, fulfillment, inspiration, mastery, wisdom, bliss, love, joy, peace and your version of success. And for those of you working on even higher aspirations, my wish is you have the non-dualistic experience of enlightenment (absolute truth, awareness, liberation), something the greatest masters have been trying to describe and teach for as long as we have been on the planet.

Entrepreneurial Success

*"If one advances confidently in the direction of his dreams,
and endeavors to live the life which he has imagined, he will
meet with success unexpected in common hours."*
Henry David Thoreau

*I*have been an entrepreneur for over 40 years, mainly because I like
being in control of my destiny. But the benefits are not just for
myself–I see entrepreneurial energy, creativity, and motivation as the
means to trigger change all over the world. If we take all the passion,
talent and ideas that entrepreneurs possess and cultivate that potential we
can build the kind of world we are all longing for.

Our materialistic lifestyle combined with our frenetic productivity is
unsustainable. We are dealing with an unprecedented depletion of species,
climate change, and global economic instability. But recently, I have seen
an awakening, or shift in consciousness about this, and a reconnection
with our deeper purpose and meaning. It is time to awaken to the limitless possibilities rather than be caught in old patterns of conditioning by
the paradigms we have held.

I love what Dr. Karl-Henrik Robèrt, Founder of The Natural Step,
said about this: "The question of reaching sustainability is not about if
we will have enough energy, food, or other resources…The question is:
Will there be enough leaders in time?"

When we bring leadership into the mix, we can accelerate the change
in the world. Leaders are selfless types with purpose and passion who can
visualize a better world in the future and are able to convince or influence
others to willingly join them on the journey because of their inspired
vision. Leaders are all about making a difference, providing momentum,

implementing new thinking and creating an atmosphere of change that improves the world.

I think that together we can create what The Pachamama Alliance describes as an environmentally sustainable, socially just, and spiritually fulfilling human presence on this planet. But to create a sustainable world, it is imperative to develop a different kind of leader: an entrepreneurial leader.

Entrepreneurs step into their power through the choices they are drawn to make. They are values driven and have learned to think differently. Entrepreneurs act as spark plugs, activating and stimulating economic activity. Some qualities of entrepreneurs stand out, especially that they:

- are risk-takers and rule breakers
- have an unquenchable desire, lifelong learners
- passionate, energetic and creative
- are obsessed with goal setting and setting outcomes
- able to encompass both excitement and fear simultaneously
- can handle uncertainty
- are decisive, highly self-motivated and self possessed
- bounce back from adversity, resilient and flexible
- identify and service unmet needs
- create value through solutions
- initiate change, are innovators
- take advantage of change
- value self-reliance and self-awareness
- strive for excellence
- know the value of mentorship/masterminds
- are highly optimistic, have a winning attitude
- deeply interested and care for others, have great people skills
- genuinely interested in developing sincere, long lasting relationships
- desire to inspire others
- do what is right and meaningful, are ethical, have high integrity
- are big picture thinkers and future driven
- see problems as opportunities
- creatively identify the solutions to problems
- want to make a difference

With persistence and determination, they create businesses or opportunities that make a difference for themselves and others. Look at the most dynamic societies in the world and you'll find the ones that have the most entrepreneurs.

> *"Patience, persistence and perspiration make*
> *an unbeatable combination for success."*
> Napoleon Hill

The name of my parent company, Potentials Within, expresses what I feel: each of us has the potential to be whatever we desire, and the answers are within each of us. There is a unique expression within you that is meant to contribute to the world. When we internalize the Universal/Eternal/ Cosmic Laws, we are more in harmony with our personal and spiritual growth, our values, vision, purpose and our destiny. When we act on our uniqueness and on what we have learned, we become a natural entrepreneur, and are expressing our gifts to this planet. We are leaving our legacy.

Now let's focus a bit more on the aspect of success. This is usually what entrepreneurs are looking for in their business ventures. But there are as many ways to describe success as there are people. According to new thought leader Earl Nightingale, "Success is the progressive realization of a worthy goal or ideal." Another expert on success, Napoleon Hill, proclaims that, "Success is the attainment of your definite chief aim without violating the rights of other people."

The Law of Success has a bottom line: Real success comes when your results benefit your fellow human beings and the world is enriched. Yes, your personal goals and aims are important, but advancement in all areas is the highest purpose of this Law. True entrepreneurial success has the same standard.

The important thing is that every one of us has our own individual definition based on our values, desires, goals, dreams, worthy ideals, life vision, intentions and aspirations. We could say our external success would encompass achievement, productivity, and making things happen while our inner success boils down to our feelings like joy, contentment and fulfillment. In our journey as spiritual beings, success encompasses not only material wealth but also sound physical health, fulfilling relationships, meaningful friendships, the joy of self-expression, freedom from negative emotions, the capacity to understand people, self-mastery and being in the flow.

My wish is that you study the 30 Laws of Flow in this book, use them to re-create your world and re-design your success, and become one of those conscious, values driven entrepreneurial leaders that our world so desperately needs.

Here's to your success while being in the flow!

Four Fundamentals

I have chosen these four fundamental principles out of all that I have learned from hundreds of courses. They are essential to understand in order to get the best results when working with the 30 Laws of Flow to magnify your flow of time, money and productivity.

As you read these Fundamentals, try not to analyze them too greatly right now. Just let them sink in and get a feeling for the overall picture of the relationship of body and mind and spirit. Later, you can go more deeply and refer to many more readings that I'll cite, but for now, just get the main ideas.

1. Our Three Planes Of Existence–Understanding Who We Really Are
2. The Activity Of The Mind
3. Awareness And Working With Our Filters
4. The Potential And Wisdom Of Our Physical Body (Our Vehicle)

1. Our Three Planes Of Existence–Understanding Who We Really Are

Science is exploring the field of consciousness more and more these days. The more research is done, the more evidence arises that our lives are not as simple as a physical body with a physical brain. We actually live on three planes of existence simultaneously. We are **spiritual** beings living in a **physical** body and creating through our **mental** awareness and **emotional** states. Another way to say this is that we have very specialized tools with which to create, direct, and shape our experience of living. These include our physical body, our mental/emotional capabilities, and our spiritual potential.

As we might expect, our physical body is the level of awareness with which we are most familiar. It is our vehicle and is an instrument of the mind. We know our body largely through the systems that work together to keep everything functioning: the circulatory, digestive, endocrine, immune, lymphatic, muscular, reproductive, urinary, respiratory, skeletal, and the nervous system. We—are very aware of our sense organs: sight, smell, taste, touch, and hearing. We have been programmed to navigate through our world with these senses.

But if we look at our bodies energetically, there is evidence that we have enough energy potential to light a large city for nearly a week. (If you have seen the movie *The Secret*, you might remember Bob Proctor giving this analogy.)

The mental aspect is our connection point, manifesting the invisible into physical reality. Even though none of us have ever seen the mind, we see the manifestations of the mind daily. We access our thoughts through our mind. Our mind is the conduit between the invisible and the visible, and allows us access to the infinite potential of the Universal Consciousness. By using our mind to create, we tap into all kinds of possibilities or probabilities of this unified field. Since everything lies in potential in this quantum field, knowing how to access it and what to do with it has enormous implications. (More on this in the chapter—The Quantum of Flow.)

Connected to our mental capacity, our emotions are our guidance system. Our feelings describe the conscious awareness of the vibration which we are in, and can be used as guideposts. They let us know if we are on the right track or not. They can act as motivators that move us into action, or depressors that keep us stuck.

Emotions work in conjunction with thoughts. I used to be confused about which came first but then, when I studied neurochemistry, I learned that a thought triggers a chemical which is experienced as an emotion.

Thought ⇨ Neurochemical sequence ⇨ Experience of Emotion (Sensation)

That creates a sensation and the brain then looks back through our memory to find a pattern that is similar to what we are feeling. That's how we label what we are feeling.

Emotion (Sensation) ⇨ Memory ⇨ Interpretation/Meaning (Energized Thought)

What can happen is that the feeling becomes so ingrained that we think the *feeling* is the driving force and it affects our thinking. We tend to think the way we feel and feel the way we think. So for many of us, the emotions can be a stumbling block to growth until the role they play is fully understood. Think of them as feedback as to whether you are headed in the right direction or not.

When we are feeling what we label as negative emotions, that is guidance that we are not headed in the right direction. On the other hand we can use our feelings to attract what it is that we desire. When we generate the feeling of what we desire the Universe is energetically matching our vibration using the Law of Attraction. Basically you want to fall in love with what you desire. When we are in love, the Universe turns desires into reality faster. Learn to select thoughts that make you feel good. Successful people have become skilled at habituating good feelings.

Finally, our spiritual aspect, sometimes referred to as our super-consciousness, the Truth or Absolute Awareness, is the hardest part to describe in words. It is the part of us with no form. It is the state prior to thoughts. It is the level of awareness that we are becoming more mindful of in this new age of consciousness. It is who we really are. Our responsibility is to become aware of this higher aspect of ourselves and kindle its presence to develop a new reality. Being aware that this higher plane of awareness is available to you 24/7.

2. The Activity Of The Mind

Even though the mind has no single physical location, many people are aware that there are basically three states of mind: the subconscious, the conscious, and the super-conscious.

The **subconscious** governs the body/mind functions. It functions in every cell of our body. This is the part of our mind that is the power center. It does not recognize time or space, only vibrations. It processes images not words. The subconscious mind has no ability to reject a thought. It accepts everything that is impressed upon it. It is totally deductive. It operates on autopilot. It never sleeps; it is always on duty recording everything. In fact, it turns out that the subconscious mind cannot tell the difference between that which is real in your life and that which you are imagining. Knowing that one simple thing has made the difference between star athlete winners and those who never quite get there, because many times it is the vivid, repetitive imagining of a course or a move or a routine that provides the winning edge.

The subconscious is also referred to as our emotional center, or our feeling mind. It operates in an orderly manner, by Law. This is where our paradigms and our habitual behavior patterns are held. (These paradigms will continue to express themselves without any conscious assistance until they are replaced with new paradigms. Their strategy is to keep you safe, comfortable and secure. Can you see how important it might be to know what paradigms may be currently operating? These show up in great abundance when we get out of our comfort zone going toward our goals.)

The **conscious** governs body/mind actions. This is the part of the mind that has the ability to think and can originate thought. It is connected to all our senses. Through our senses we connect to the external world and it is reflected back to our conscious mind as an image. It can accept or reject any idea to which it is exposed. It can make choices. This is where our free will lies as well as both inductive and deductive thinking. We have six intellectual faculties that give us our creative ability:

- Reasoning
- Will or Concentration
- Perception
- Memory
- Intuition
- Imagination

These creative abilities assist us in connecting to our **super-consciousness**; the part of us that is self-aware, our true self, the connection with our spiritual nature. Self- awareness can encourage us to ask questions, to reflect on our behavior, to look at the larger picture and invite the answers to come to us. Our answers will come from the true self in this awareness. With this awareness, we can pay attention to the one who is aware, the observer. The witness that is the reflection of the real. When we are self-aware, reality shifts and we can start to make better choices. Becoming self-aware empowers us to make more wholesome choices for our highest good.

The super-consciousness governs body/mind and the mental/spiritual. This is the part of the mind, along with the subconscious mind, that is connected to the collective Consciousness, the Unified Field, the Universal Mind, the Ultimate Awareness. When we tune in here, it is easier to feel the connection with pure awareness, The All.

3. Awareness and Working With Our Filters

Awareness is the ability to perceive, to feel, or to be conscious of objects, events, or sensory patterns. Self awareness is the capacity for introspection and having a clear perception of our personality, including strengths, weaknesses, behavioral patterns, beliefs, thoughts, motivation, filters, and emotional reactions.

Old existing paradigms can block awareness, so we need to work on expanding our awareness daily.

Current thinking dictates there are seven levels of awareness and depending on where we are in our lives at any given time, we may bounce back and forth between levels.

We start with the animalistic or stimulus-response level of awareness where we react to everything and live at the fight or flight level or survival level.

Then we go to robot school and get taught to follow the masses, to conform, to do what everyone else is doing. We are anxious what others think of us. We are concerned with self preservation, security, and safety. We don't ask for what we want, we are afraid to make mistakes, and have low self esteem. We blame others for our results, give up our power, and stay locked into a poverty mentality. This is our second level of awareness.

Then we desire something greater, to be, do, or have more than our current circumstances. We want to break away from the masses and become an individual and aspire to express our uniqueness. We begin to dream and leave our comfort zone. We move into action because we have the faith to move toward our desires and utilize our will to get there. This is our third and fourth levels of awareness.

Our fifth level of awareness involves discipline, the ability to give ourselves a command and follow it. This awareness is necessary to break away from the mass level of consciousness. This denotes staying the course regardless of what the masses are doing and/or saying. This means perfecting new behavior patterns that turn into productive success habits. This awareness involves intense focus and commitment.

With this awareness we go to the next level of awareness called experience. With this level of awareness real learning takes place. We become aware the answers are within. Our own abilities are reinforced. We have new ideas that lead to new actions that change our results. We know how to make decisions. We are aware of our value system and learn to ask effective questions. We can learn to use our mental faculties constructively,

On the mastery level of awareness we respond to events and circumstances and know that whatever the challenge or question we need an answer to, we will receive it. There is a calmness of mind and unity recognition at this awareness. We have an expanded perspective and openness to new possibilities and realize we live in an abundant universe. We understand the laws and know how to utilize the laws of energy. We are no longer controlled by habitual patterns or paradigms. We operate from belief in the outcome when setting goals and are quite effective at attracting success, wealth, and resources. We have the ability to choose, know we create our reality and take full responsibility. Life just seems to flow here.

Now let's become aware of some of our filters. There are many filters but only a few will be addressed in this book. A filter is anything that the mind uses to:

- Sort out the entirety of information available to the senses,
- Choose some of it but not all of it,
- Give the resulting subset of data a particular meaning, and
- Act on it (or not) accordingly.

The one filter that is seen most prominently is our own personality. Personality is defined as a dynamic and organized set of characteristics possessed by individuals that uniquely influence our cognitions, emotions, motivations, and behaviors in various situations. It reveals aspects of our character or psychological makeup.

Our personality is made up of how we think, act and feel consistently. It really is a habit. The word personality originates from the Latin *persona*, which means mask. What does it mask? Who we really are–spiritual beings.

On the physical level, we reaffirm our personality when we think the same thoughts today as we did yesterday, perform the same actions, and live by the same emotions. We process about 60,000–75,000 thoughts in a day. Of those thoughts, about 96% are the same thoughts we had the day before. So the same thoughts will lead to the same choices. The same choices will create the same behaviors. The same behaviors will produce the same experiences or results. The same experiences will create the same emotions. Those familiar emotions will drive the same thoughts over and over again, and this finite relationship in our brain becomes a kind of signature or a pattern. We call it an identity.

For the first third of our lives we put all our attention on the external world as we are conditioned to learn through our senses. During this phase of our lives we keep creating more of a personality identity by identifying with our external world. This becomes the facade, the illusion, and the image we project to the world. So we begin to create a gap: how our personalities appear to the world versus our spiritual nature, (who we really are). There is now a conflict that continues until we start to feel the onset of uncertainty or discontent. Only then will we begin the process of change.

When we start the transformation of expressing our inner selves in the external world, we become more open, removing the filters and masks and letting spirit move through us. A sure sign of this is when we are happy for no reason, feeling content, peaceful–it is coming from within us, we are no longer separate from it, and we are in a different state of consciousness, in the flow.

NOTE: There are wonderful tools out there that assess personality, give insight into understanding ourselves, and help enhance our journey of self-discovery. I share some of my favorite ones in the 30 Laws of Flow section and in the suggested resources list. Be sure to check out:

The Wisdom of the Enneagram: The Complete Guide to Psychological and Spiritual Growth for the Nine Personality Types by Russ Hudson and Don Richard Riso

Conative Connection: Uncovering the Link Between Who You Are and How You Perform by Kathy Kolbe

Power vs. Force: The Hidden Determinants of Human Behavior by David R. Hawkins

Breaking the Habit of Being Yourself by Dr. Joe Dispenza

The Success Puzzle and The Goal Achiever by Bob Proctor to learn more about your intellectual faculties.

Another powerful filter can be our attitude. Our consciousness is the first place we get to choose our attitude. There is a creative power flowing into our consciousness. It is neither positive nor negative. We build images with this power and we can choose either positive or negative images. The image we choose is expressed through our feelings and actions. If our choice is a negative one, it will filter everything around us as being negative and we will experience that on all levels. Once we make the decision to change it into a positive one, everything will appear positive and we will be vibrating on a higher frequency. Ultimately, it is our choice, but sometimes our current attitude can feel as if it is set in stone forever. The key thing to understand is that it is NOT set, and can actually be changed in mere moments with a decision to change.

Another serious filter is paying attention to *only* our five senses and thinking that our physical world is all that there is. The invisible aspect of this world penetrates and permeates everything. To quote Wallace Wattles in his magnificent book "The Science of Getting Rich,"

"Every man has the natural and inherent power to think what he wants to think, but it requires far more effort to do so than it does to think the thoughts which are suggested by appearances. To think according to appearance is easy; to think truth regardless of appearances is laborious, and requires the expenditure of more power than any other work man is called upon to perform."

To hold an image using the invisible "thinking stuff" and keep the image in our mind until it manifests into the physical may be the hardest work to do in this human form. But it is worth all the effort to go beyond our physical senses and express our creativity into the physical realm.

To do this we need to break the cycle of letting our present results control our thoughts, which in turn controls our feelings and those feelings control our actions which produces more of the same results. That cycle is totally dependent on our sensory world and once we become aware and build a picture of what we want in our minds and get emotionally involved with it, we won't let the present results influence our new image.

Our subconscious mind is full of paradigms—those complex and habitual memorized behavioral patterns, emotional reactions, assumptions, values, perceptions, attitudes, beliefs or scripts that can act as *filters* to our experiences. Generally they are other people's habits, instilled in us by our parents, teachers or caregivers and passed on to us genetically from one generation to another. Paradigms are deeply entrenched habits in our subconscious and guide our behavior and how we make choices. Our paradigms or beliefs control our perception, effectiveness, productivity, our ability to earn money, and much more. They even control our logic. What we don't realize is that our subconscious mind operates this programming for us approximately 96% of the time. It is running the show, so our lives are created mostly from our subconscious programming on autopilot. It is like an internal map or blueprint that has to match the outside world. If we are not cultivating new habits, the old ones run automatically (even without our knowing it).

*"The mind moves in the direction of our currently
dominant thoughts."*
Earl Nightingale

When our conscious and subconscious mind are not in sync, we could be *consciously* thinking a positive thought but on the *subconscious* level we could be emotionally involved with a pre-programmed negative thought or habit. This conflict shows up as not getting the results we wanted to achieve. For example, if we are picturing being wealthy and feeling how joyous it would be to have that experience, we are attracting the feeling of wealth and abundance to us. But if we are picturing being wealthy and at the same time feeling disconcerted on the subconscious feeling level because of an existing paradigm that asserts that we don't deserve it, then our existing paradigm is pushing the prosperity experience away. The reason our existing paradigm wins is because it's job is to keep us safe, comfortable and secure. The vibrations we are sending out to the universe are contradictory, and contradictory energy waves, in effect, cancel each other out. Our conscious thinking and our subconscious feeling have to be a match in order to experience wealth. **In the game of manifestation, the vibration held most consistently wins.**

To learn more how our existing paradigms keep us safe is through understanding a mechanism called *Psycho-Cybernetics* developed by Dr. Maxwell Maltz. "Psycho" relates to the mind and "cybernetics" is the science of self-regulating systems. Maltz found that the subconscious mind acts like a cybernetic mechanism operating automatically, just like the set temperature on a thermostat. This system causes us to consistently behave the way we do and will continue to keep bringing us back to the familiar, safe, secure, comfortable place or our set point. All this happens without our conscious awareness.

When we set a new goal, our existing fixed habits (or beliefs) direct this mechanism to measure the deviation between our set point (where we are comfortable and safe) and where we want to go with our new goal (which can activate fear of the unknown). The fear will trigger this cybernetic mechanism to measure the deviation from the safe place or set point. It sends a message to our conscious mind and tells us what to think and simultaneously sends a message to our subconscious mind and tells us what to feel. This directive corrects the course and brings us back to our safe set point and stops our forward progression towards our goal which alleviates the fear. Our focus changes and we start to think of all the reasons why we can't or shouldn't go after the goal. Without re-setting this system, nothing will change. It is important to become aware of this cybernetic mechanism and understand its powerful influence over us.

> *"Of what use to make heroic vows of amendment,*
> *if the same old lawbreaker is going to keep them."*
> Ralph Waldo Emerson

The key to reset this autopilot of our subconscious is using our imagination with repetition to create a *new* set point. Using images and sounds, we can reprogram old paradigms and develop a new self-image or new set point that automatically guides us to what we desire. Once we are at this new set point, there is no fear attached to it as the awareness has expanded so it is easier to obtain the goal. Imagination is one of our most treasured gifts. With imagination we can change even what we believe to be real. Through our imagination we can access infinite possibilities and create the image we desire.

I know it might seem overwhelming to attempt to reprogram everything you've learned that doesn't serve you very well. But the beautiful thing about all these filters is that they can guide and teach us and are valuable tools for self-discovery. Becoming more aware of the filters we use that cloud our "vision" helps us learn about ourselves and others. There are other filters not addressed here, such as your values system, but once you decide to explore your inner world, there are many tools available to aid in that process. Ultimately dissolving our filters enrich us as we become stronger and more courageous in the process and lead us back to who we really are. As Ralph Waldo Emerson said, "Don't be pushed by your problems. Be led by your dreams."

4. The Potential and Wisdom Of Our Physical Body (Our Vehicle)

Our body and brain are the most sophisticated pieces of equipment known to man. John Assaraf says they make a super computer look like a plaything! To understand exactly how we really function at every level increases our potential and our results. We have amazing abilities and just need to tap into them.

We are blessed with a brain, spinal cord and peripheral nervous system that makes up our central nervous system. The nervous system is our body's decision and communication center. Together they control every part of our daily life, from breathing and blinking, to helping us memorize facts. Sensory nerves gather information from the environment, send that information to the spinal cord, which then speeds the message to the brain. The brain then makes sense of that message and fires off a response. Motor neurons deliver the instructions from the brain to the rest of our body. The spinal cord, made of a bundle of nerves running up and down the spine, is similar to a expressway, speeding messages to and from the brain at every second.

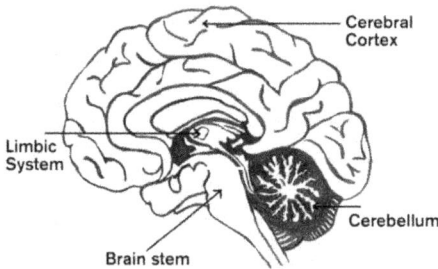

Different parts of the brain have their own functions to keep the body running smoothly. The basic structures are the cerebrum (which contains the cerebral cortex), the cerebellum, the limbic system and the brain stem.

Of particular interest to goal setters is the reticular activating system (known as the RAS). It is a primitive network of nerve cells and fibers that is part of the mammalian brain located in the brain stem. The RAS has two portions: one is the

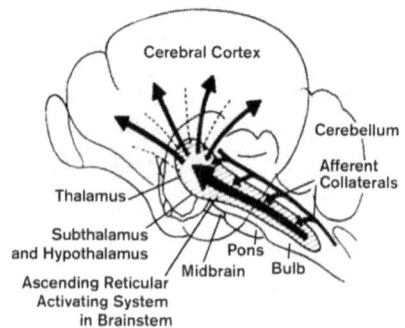

ascending RAS which is connected to the cortex, hypothalamus and the thalamus, and the other one is the descending RAS which is connected to the nerves. Both play a very important role in the human body.

Perhaps the most important function of the RAS is the control of consciousness; it is believed to control the ability to consciously focus attention on something. In addition, the RAS acts as a filter for all of the sensory inputs that we receive, helping to prevent the senses from being overloaded. The RAS decides what is and what is not important to us and what we need to pay attention to. The "filter" sits between the subconscious and conscious minds, and is programmed by the conscious mind. It is this ability to *program the filter* that makes the RAS so important in helping us to maintain focus and to achieve a goal.

Now let's look at our brain from the perspective of how the brain allows us to go from thinking, to doing, to being. Remember the Universe responds to the vibration of who we are being, not what we are thinking or what we are doing. I will divide the brain into three parts in order to show how each part of the brain contributes to the process of change, and how we can "change our mind" by literally changing our brain. (For more information on this, check out Dr. Joe Dispenza's work and books and be sure to read *Buddha's Brain: The Practical Neuroscience of Happiness, Love & Wisdom* by Rick Hanson and Richard Mendius.)

What is called the "first brain" is the neocortex consisting of the grey matter, our intellect, thinking, or analytical brain. It loves to gather information from our environment. When we acquire new information we make a new connection in our thinking brain. Then we take that knowledge and we apply it. This means we will have to modify our behavior in some way and do something differently. When we change our actions we get a new experience.

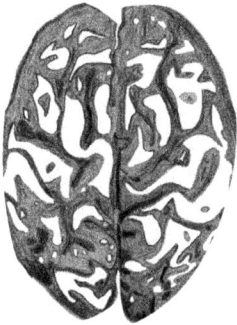

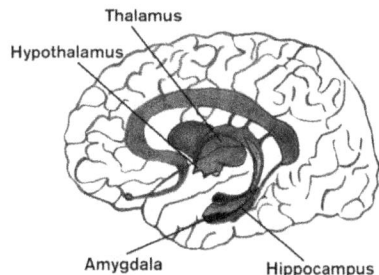

Thalamus

Hypothalamus

Amygdala   Hippocampus

Then the experience signals the "second brain" called the limbic brain. (This is also referred to as the emotional brain or the chemical brain. It contains the thalamus, hypothalamus, the hippocampus, and the amygdala.)

When we can think about what we are thinking about, it means we have a certain degree of self-awareness. We are conscious of the observer part. We become conscious of our subconscious or unconscious habits and behaviors. We notice the feelings and emotions that keep us connected to the past. Using our forebrain, we can modify our state of being to create a better experience. This is best done through meditation. Meditation is a great way to bring about a shift in your relationship with yourself.

When we are observing, we are no longer the automatic program, we are the *observer* of that program. We begin to separate ourselves from our subjective mind. We begin to objectify our subjective self. We begin to silence the connections of the old self image and old paradigms and weaken the connections. We then remind ourselves of all our new knowledge (goal) and begin to plan our new behaviors. We mentally rehearse using our imagination and positive emotions and begin to plan our actions. We make our brain work on the new sequences and patterns (habits) and this, literally, changes our mind. We are no longer observing our life from the same level of mind, we are experiencing a new feeling and it is no longer just a philosophy, we are truly experiencing it. (Remember the subconscious mind cannot tell the difference between what is real and what is imagined.)

Once we experience our new behavior over and over again and our body memorizes this new behavior or pattern, then our mind and body are working together and we are in a new state of being. (Again, notice the importance of repetition until a new behavior is memorized or the new goal achieved.)

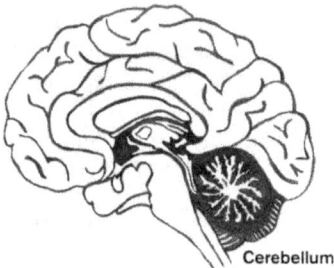

We then activate our "third brain", the cerebellum, where our habits and our skills are wired. With developed

Cerebellum

habits and skills, we have done it so many times we don't have to think about it any longer. We know that we do it, but we don't know how we do it, because it is innate in us. It is automatic, it is subconscious, it is second nature, it is who we think we are.

When we are in that state of being we could say that we have memorized an internal new chemical order. At that level of integration or internal order when nothing outside can move us from it, we are now mastering that state of being, and it becomes our new pattern, habit or paradigm. When it becomes so habitual we are no longer conscious of it and it resides in our subconscious.

We have gone from thinking, to doing, to being, all by using our brain as the template for this journey of change. I know it might not be easy to follow at first, but if you re-read it a few times, it will become clearer. The bottom line is that our brain can change any currently held thought, value, belief, habit, assumption, pattern or paradigm into one that gives us better results. And the good news is that we can make that change automatic with repetition.

More good news for us: an enormous amount of recent research known as neural plasticity or brain plasticity has revealed that the brain never stops changing and adjusting and is constantly revising itself. Neuroscience has now proved that we can change our brain just by thinking differently. The brain has the ability to change–chemically, physically, and functionally–throughout life.

In fact, the brain changes *physically* every time we learn something new. When we are changed by new thoughts, new dreams, new choices, new lessons, new experiences, the brain reorganizes itself. The neural pathways in the brain are reorganized or re-wired. The best news of all is that we can develop new "wires" (neural pathways) with repetition of information. What a relief–we are not doomed by our genetics, and we can play an active, conscious role in redesigning our brains and our bodies!

In the area of genetics the scientific community has been studying what is called epigenetics. Previously it was thought our genes were the molecular units of heredity and we were predestined to what we inherited. It turns out that genetic data (the genome) has a outer expression called epigenome. The epigenome consists of chemical compounds that modify, or mark, the genome causing the genes to express themselves differently. They can tightly wrap inactive genes making them unreadable and they can relax active genes making them more accessible. These modifications do not change the DNA sequence, but instead, they affect how cells "read" genes.

What is interesting is that epigenetic tags react to signals from the outside world. Now research is showing gene expression can be changed by habit, beliefs, attitudes, thoughts, emotions, diet, lifestyle, even unconscious beliefs through the epigenome. The epigenome is flexible and modifies gene expression in response to our environment. With this new scientific breakthrough, it appears we can become masters of our genetic makeup rather than victims of it.

When we begin to lift our energy, we begin to signal genes in new ways because it is new information. Our body will re-organize in a matter of moments to create a new brain pattern. This changes our state of being. I learned from Dr. Joe Dispenza that the receptor sites on the outside of our cells are 100 times more sensitive to frequency than they are to chemistry. If existing neural pathways do not have a purpose, they will not survive. Ineffective or weak connections are cut off and this allows the brain to adapt itself to its environment along with the new wiring thanks to the epigenetic tags.

Okay now.... Let's take a moment. I know our brains have been stretched in this section to see how our thoughts interface with our magnificent vehicle called the body. There is a wisdom we can utilize here and just reminding you to breathe right now is one way to capture some of the potential you have within.

My whole point here was to show you the scientifically verifiable ways we actually change our reality. To change our mind we need the brain to work on new signatures and new patterns or combinations. When we take a conscious role in redesigning our lives, we are also redesigning our brains and even our genetic expression.

Take another deep breath as now it's time to open to these possibilities and implement some of what you have learned.

"You were born with potential.
You were born with goodness and trust.
You were born with ideals and dreams.
You were born with greatness.
You were born with wings.
You are not meant for crawling, so don't.
You have wings.
Learn to use them and fly."
Rumi

The 30 Day Plan
Implementation Ideas

---

*T*his book is a collection of the wisdom that I have studied, practiced, and learned from over the years. Much of the material for these Laws has come from profound ancient texts, old classics, new brain research, and the insightful, life-changing programs of Bob Proctor, Mary Morrissey and other new thought leaders.

The 30 Laws of Flow embrace the fundamentals as outlined in:

- the 7 Laws of Energy, (some people call these the "Predictable Constants"),
- the 12 Universal Laws (the Spiritual, Eternal, Cosmic Laws that have been passed along from ancient wisdom, although there is some disagreement about how many of these Laws there really are, and these subordinate Laws really require the 7 Laws of Energy to function),
- the 11 Truth Principles from Raymond Holliwell (referred to as the 11 Forgotten Laws) and
- *Your Invisible Power* by Genevieve Behrend.

The important thing is that these Laws exist whether you are aware of them or not, or if you choose to apply them or not. You are, in fact, always immersed in the 30 Laws of Flow because they are integral to life. They form the foundation of the Universe as we know it, and are like the rainbow colors, they all blend together and work in concert. You cannot be separated from them, even if you wanted to be! It is part of being human.

But NOT knowing about these Laws causes you to manifest by default. Most people are not familiar with what the Laws are or how they work. Ignorance of these Laws can be the reason you experience debt, dissatisfaction with your business, unfulfilled relationships, and even ill health. So by choosing to be a deliberate creator and taking action every day, you will be learning how to move energy and make necessary changes in your life. Especially if you are an entrepreneur, the more you *consciously* take on the insights of each Law, and the suggested applications in this book, the more you will notice the benefits in the new results you will get, specifically in your flow of time, money and productivity.

The Universal/Eternal/Cosmic Laws must be *applied* if we are to consciously create what we desire, such as a new relationship, more money, more time, a new business, or more success.

Choose the implementation method that's best for your lifestyle and your needs. The first time you go through the program, do it with no expectations on yourself. This initial journey will simply acquaint your subconscious mind with the basic ideas and concepts; repeating the process later will bring deeper benefits. Repetition is the key to all learning. You can:

1. Read it quickly to get an overview and choose the Law you are most drawn to in order to solve a problem you currently have.
2. Open this book at random to any page, and dive deeply into the study and practice of the Law you have chosen.
3. Let your intuition guide you to a page when you feel like you need a message and explore whatever Law shows up on that page.
4. Choose to integrate some of the daily success applications into your day.
5. Decide to do the 30 Day plan, taking one day for each Law. (For more information on how to customize your plan, visit **www.30LawsofFlow.com.**

If you are starting the 30 Day Plan

Congratulations! You are about to embark on a journey of self discovery, developing habits that lead to greater success in both your personal life and in your business. The rewards will be priceless.

To make this plan work best, you will need a journal book, a quiet space, and some time every day dedicated to the applications you choose to apply for each Law of Flow. Each morning, after waking up, I would suggest reading (or listening to) the *meditation* for that day. (As an option, you can purchase the meditations I have recorded as MP3s.) But this is not required. Yes, listening to them is a very pleasant and powerful way to re-condition your thinking for success, but reading them is effective too. Just make sure you have set aside some quiet time so that you won't be distracted.

My recommendation is depending on whether your focus is personal or business related, that the meditation, gratitude, exercise and hydration become the essential core success rituals/habits/practices. Then tailor your choices to the particular goal you are working toward as to whether you focus on a life insight, a mindful practice or a success strategy.

Let's just summarize about what you will be doing each day. Each day's Law provides the following applications or daily success rituals/habits/practices:

1. a Universal/Eternal/Cosmic Law to contemplate—whether you are aware of these Laws or not, they are still in operation. The more you familiarize yourself with these Laws, the more you will experience harmony, grace, ease and flow in your life. Feel free to take a sentence or two and make affirmations out of them to really cement the energy of each Law.

2. an illustration of the Law—this will be a demonstration of either how these Laws have impacted me personally, or how I have learned from them, or a thought on how they can enhance entre-preneurial success.

3. a meditation to read—meditation is an important habit for improving focus, concentration, clarity and attention span, as well as having a calming effect. Benefits include: relieving stress, trauma and anxiety, calming the amygdala (the fight or flight trigger), counter-acting aging, relieving depression, reducing insomnia, improving the immune system, increasing energy, improving communication skills, enhancing empathy, improving health, being more present,

refreshing the mind, clearing the mental clutter and getting into a more expansive state. Meditation also introduces you to your inner self, your witness, your observer. Great moments of inspiration and creativity can come from those still spaces during meditation where you can connect with your inner guidance. (Ultimately though, through practice, you want to get to the place where you leave your thoughts behind. That is when you will find ultimate happiness and be in the flow continuously.)

4. time for gratitude—gratitude connects you with creative thought and brings you closer to the source energy. Gratitude aligns you with abundance and increases your faith.

5. an idea for physical exercise—exercise boosts energy, improves mood, reduces stress, releases endorphins, improves self-confidence, boosts brainpower, sharpens your memory and increases your creativity. (Feel free to disregard the suggestions if you are already in an established exercise regime.)

6. hydration for our vehicle (the body)—water is important for the brain. It improves blood flow and oxygen to the brain, improves memory, counteracts mental fatigue, and maintains the balance of body fluids. Water also energizes muscles and keep joints more lubricated, helps your skin look good, improves the quality of sleep, keeps your bowels moving and aids kidney function, and eliminates toxins. Bottom line, when you are hydrated you have more energy and it boosts your creativity.

7. a life insight—these insights promote further understanding and application of the true nature of the Universal Laws.

8. a mindful practice—this practice is to counter your daily frenzy of multi-tasking and bring you to a centered mindful place. A place of presence. Being with your body as it is with no judgment. It's important to take time out for yourself, even if it is just for a moment. When you do, you are more efficient, alert and can attract your strongest results.

9. a success strategy—these strategies or actions are some of the best ones that successful entrepreneurs apply in the process of growth and continuous improvement. When you employ these strategies,

you are supporting the goals or the vision you have. You will notice that the focus is on the "inner game" of success. (But remember to integrate the Law of Action with these strategies.) You will be encouraged to get an accountability partner for many of these applications.

10. additional resources to explore—to further your investigation and inquiry. This list is by no means complete, as you'll find out when you dive into any of these subjects on your own. (Also check out the suggested resources in the back of the book.)

You will notice quite a few components in this program are related to self-care. Self-care is the foundation for all personal growth. It is about taking care of our physical, mental, emotional and spiritual needs so we can nurture ourselves and reconnect to source. See it as honoring yourself and know that developing new habits is the groundwork to reprogramming your subconscious. The whole idea here is that you are focusing on training your nervous system and liberating yourself from your programmed responses. So make the time and space to enjoy the process. It can be life-changing.

For some of you, this material may not be new, but it may give you a different angle on familiar principles, or create a connection that you hadn't seen before. For others, it may be completely new, so I encourage you to take a deep breath, step into the unknown, and try each of the meditations and various applications just for fun. See what appeals to you, what works for you immediately, and what takes a bit longer to learn. But keep it light and enjoy the process as it unfolds.

By the end of this daily plan of success rituals/habits/practices, you will have had a taste of each of the Laws, and had some experience of how the Laws operate in your life. You will have practiced creating new habits in the areas of journaling, meditation, gratitude and exercise. You will be more familiar with Universal/Eternal/Cosmic Laws, both quantum and physical, and more able to create what you really want or desire and magnify your flow of time, money and productivity.

Some of the Laws you will be more drawn to than others, some you will really love, and others you may feel are a bit more of a challenge.

But overall, the key benefit of this process is that it enhances your aware-ness of the 30 Laws of Flow, simply by noticing and observing how aligned you are with each Law. The more you practice these insights of alignment, the more you can work with them, not against them.

Once you finish the first 30 days, start over again! This plan is designed to be followed over and over again, enhancing your results every time you use it. Remember, discover, wonder, explore, ponder, live with it, love it, grow into it, grow with it, make it your own. Go for the flow!

> *"Live your life as though your every act were*
> *to become a universal law."*
> Immanuel Kant

I would love to hear about your successes using this 30 Day Plan! Feel free to share your results with me on The 30 Laws of Flow Facebook page or through my website: **www.30LawsofFlow.com**. There you will find out how you can be supported through the "Going For The Flow" programs.

I must say, the most *ineffective* way to use this program is to do it once and imagine that, just because you've heard and read all the words, you've gotten the message. (Believe me, I've done this too many times over the years, so I know!) With each repetition, you will hear it or see it from a slightly a different perspective, because truly, you will be slightly different yourself. I have to thank Bob Proctor for demonstrating the importance of repetition to me once and for all. My life has changed radically, thanks to this one concept.

Basically, your subconscious mind needs the magic of repetition to complete the act of reprogramming negative paradigms, habits, thoughts with positive ones. You've been getting negative messages for so many years, and a one-time encounter of any positive message just isn't going to do the job. With repetition, your brain literally develops new neural pathways. Regularly applying these new ideas, insights and applications, your subconscious mind can absorb them and process them so that even-tually these intentional positive messages will outweigh the unintentional negative ones. Your thinking will change, and your results will change as you magnify your flow of time, money and productivity.

So, enjoy whatever repetition format you choose, and if it doesn't feel right for you, modify the repetition so that it works to give you the results you want. An interesting new tidbit is that the latest studies indicate that it takes an average of 66 to 90 days to create a new habit and that is only with a support system in place. Remember adopting new habits is easier with support and the discipline of consistency and this may be required to deal with your old paradigms that may tell you that it doesn't feel right, just to keep you in your current comfort zone where you feel "safe, comfortable and secure". There is no growth in this comfort zone so you may have to stretch into the repetition. One of the great secrets of transformation is simple repetition. Sometimes that repetition will be needed for over a year as the habitual patterns are so ingrained. Repetition is how we learned to walk, remember people's names, and hundreds of other things we now take for granted.

> *"We* **are** *what we repeatedly* **do**. *Excellence, then,*
> *is not an act, but a habit."*
> Aristotle

The goal here is simple: with practice, you will reprogram the old paradigms of resistance, and start to experience the natural flow inherent in the Universal Laws.

For everyone, I encourage you to surrender to the All-Knowing Great Spirit, Divine Intelligence, Universal Consciousness, The I Am That I Am, Universal Intelligence or God energy that orchestrates this dance of the universe. Let us all dance it together, consciously, and create heaven on earth because of it.

The 30 Laws of Flow:
A 30 Day Plan to Magnify
Your Flow of Time, Money
and Productivity

*T*his section will describe each Law, give you some practical illustrations as examples and some suggested applications so you can magnify your flow of time, money and productivity. Each Law is given a day, so that you can choose to make it into a consistent study. (Following a structured daily plan is the way I personally recommend to get the most possible benefit. Feel free to customize the suggested applications to the focus of your goal.)

I want to be clear that utilizing the daily rituals/habits/practices indicated with each Law will be more potent when you have something that you are focused on achieving–*a compelling vision or worthy ideal*. Something that you have fallen in love with and want to manifest.

There are three different types of goals. The first two don't count.

1. There are **goals where you are doing something you already *know* how to do.**
2. There are **goals that you already *think* you can do.** If you know how to reach your goal, the goal is not going to do for you what goals are designed to do.
3. Then there are the **goals that are your wants or desires or dreams.** They are the ones that you want to go after. These goals are going after something you've never done before. They are designed to help you expand; you grow into your goals and they cause you to draw something from yourself that you didn't even know was there. They

must inspire you and be big enough to scare you at the same time. The "how's" are going to show up step by step. In other words you are not going to know "how" they will manifest when you set them. They come from your fantasies and are originated through the effective use of your imagination. Napoleon Hill said, "Imagination is the most marvelous, miraculous, inconceivably powerful force the world has ever known." So the question is, what do you really want? Take the lid off your mind and dream. Really engage your imagination.

"The Laws Are Exact"

"The Law of your being is perpetual increase, progress, and growth, so when one good is realized, another desire for a greater good will develop; and when a higher state is reached, another and more glorious state will unfold your vision and will urge you on and on. Hence, the advancing life is the true life, the life that God intended you to live."

Adapted from Raymond Holliwell

Day 1: The Great Law–Every Thing is Energy

The Law: Everything is energy. You are energy and this energy is all around and through you.

> *"I know this world is ruled by infinite intelligence. Everything that surrounds us—everything that exists—proves that there are infinite laws behind it. There can be no denying this fact. It is mathematical in its precision."*
>
> Thomas A. Edison

My Personal Illustration

I tested out this Law by tripping over a hose in my yard. I landed face down on a concrete sidewalk and it knocked the wind out of me completely. Within moments, I felt extraordinary pain in my nose and left knee, and realized I could not walk without extreme pain. Ice and arnica treatments on the physical plane relieved some of the discomfort, but not the major part of it.

That night, still in pain, I used The Great Law: Everything is Energy. I saw my body as simply energy. I imagined connecting with the quantum field of possibilities by seeing my healthy body *prior* to tripping and falling. Throughout my meditation right then and there, I visualized a healthy body and imagined complete freedom from pain. I went to bed with the thought that I would be perfectly healthy the next day.

When I woke up, there was absolutely no pain in either my knee or nose. I still saw some bruising and felt some muscle strain in my arms, but I was free from the incapacitating pain I experienced right after the fall.

Use of the Great Law allowed me to consciously create what I wanted by knowing everything as energy and pure potentiality. This is important for an entrepreneur who wants to create new programs—it is comforting to know that there is a whole field of potentiality from which to create.

Meditation for The Great Law–Every Thing is Energy

This meditation is a key to unlocking your soul's inner knowing about this Universal Law. It is already in you, so use this time to bring it to your conscious understanding. Read the following meditation slowly.

Take a nice deep breath in through your nose and let it out through your mouth. You are going to let all the tension leave your body, and as you exhale, repeat in your mind the word: Relax.

You are in the right place at the right time. Your body and mind are in a highly creative vibration right now. Your mind and your heart are ready to receive, completely wide open. Ready to receive whatever it is that you need to know right now. You now have the best possible guidance to allow you to experience the teachings of this Law, and to gather all the important information in any way that it appears.

This quantum universe operates by exact precision and Law. Quantum physicists are now aware that everything happens by exact Law. Universal Laws, also referred to as Spiritual Laws or Eternal Laws or Cosmic Laws and closely aligned with the Laws of Nature, are the unchanging and unwavering principles that govern every aspect of the universe and are the means by which our world and the entire cosmos continues to exist, thrive and expand in a quantum field of possibilities and potentiality.

Knowing these Universal Laws is fundamental to changing the circumstances of your life so that you can consciously create your intended reality and achieve true mastery. We human beings are a part of the whole we call the Universe. The Great Law states that everything is energy. Energy is neither created nor destroyed. Change is energy's only attribute. It is either creating or disintegrating. Energy is evenly present at all places at all times and penetrates, saturates and fills the interspaces of the universe. You are energy and this energy is all around and through you. At the deepest level, nothing and no one is separate from you. You are one with this energy. When you realize that your true energy is one of pure potentiality, where there are infinite possibilities and probabilities, you align with the power that manifests everything in the universe.

Now, to finish your reading, take three deep cleansing breaths, knowing that with each breath you integrate the information you have received. Trust that this is so, and it will be.

Suggested Applications for Today's Law of Flow

Meditate Use the meditation provided for this Law by finding a quiet place to read the selection, or you can listen to the recording of it (if you have purchased the mp3's that go with this book), or use another meditation that appeals to you. (At least 15 minutes)

Gratitude Write at least three things that you are grateful for on this magnificent day. Connect to the feeling of gratitude.

Exercise Choose an exercise that gives you some joy or increases your energy. Examples are dancing, gardening, cycling, etc.

Hydrate Drink ½ ounce of pure water per pound of body weight (or 30 ml per kg). 2 glasses upon rising, 2 glasses between breakfast and lunch, 2 glasses between lunch and dinner and 2 after dinner.

Life Insight Look at nature and notice how everything operates by exact precision and Law. See how you can use the Universal Laws in your life and study and contemplate how they can help create order out of confusion.

Mindful Practice Take a moment, breathe and just be in the present. Contemplate and explore the world of quantum physics. There are many books and extensive materials on the internet, so explore and see what appeals to you. My first introduction to quantum physics was the book "The Dancing Wu Li Masters" (see resources below). Another one of my favorites is not a book at all, but a film: "What The Bleep Do We Know?"

Success Strategy Ralph Waldo Emerson said "We become what we think about all day long." Contemplate or meditate on this critical statement for success. Find a copy of Earl Nightingale's book, *The Strangest Secret: How to Live the Life You Desire* and find the quote that matches Emerson's quote. See yourself already in possession of the goal you are working on, assuming the feeling that you already have it.

Resources *Dancing Wu Li Masters: An Overview of the New Physics* by Gary Zukav

Quantum Physics For Dummies by Steven Holzner

The Biology of Belief: Unleashing the Power of Consciousness, Matter & Miracles by Bruce H. Lipton

Day 2: The Law Of Vibration

The Law: Everything in the universe, including you, is pure energy vibrating at different frequencies. You are energy vibrating at a specific vibratory rate. Your vibration will attract like vibrations to you. (Day 12: Law of Attraction) Learn to manage your vibration, and you will see what you bring into your life.

> *"If you want to find the secrets of the universe,*
> *think in terms of energy, frequency and vibration."*
> Nikola Tesla

My Personal Illustration

Many years ago, not yet aware of the Law of Vibration, I was in a foul mood and out driving. I parked the car in a parking lot and paid what I thought was needed for the length of my appointment. Later, I came out to find a parking ticket–I hadn't paid the correct amount. This increased my foul mood. Within minutes of pulling out of the parking lot, I was pulled over by a policeman because I did not see that there was no left turn during the hours that I had just turned. So I received *another* ticket! It took me a few years to realize that I had attracted these unhappy events because they mirrored my vibration that day.

Another day, I woke up feeling great and excited to experience the day. I went to an event and since my vibration was what I describe as "being in the flow," I attracted interesting people and was asked to go to another event spontaneously. The next event was a potluck and, consistent with this vibratory state, I already had a dish prepared and ready to go for this spontaneous invitation. Being in the flow that day, led me to meeting new people who in the future would lead me into new business ventures.

Vibration is vitally important and is the power behind the Law of Attraction. As an entrepreneur, this Law is essential for your business to become successful. People are attracted to people who are vibrating at a frequency that is attractive to be around.

Meditation for The Law of Vibration

This meditation is a key to unlocking your soul's inner knowing about this Universal Law. It is already in you, so use this time to bring it to your conscious understanding. Read the following meditation slowly.

Take a nice deep breath in through your nose and let it out through your mouth. You are going to let all the tension leave your body, and as you exhale, repeat in your mind the word: Relax.

You are in the right place at the right time. Your body and mind are in a highly creative vibration right now. Your mind and your heart are ready to receive whatever it is that you need to know. You have the best possible guidance to allow you to experience the teachings of this Law, and to gather all the important information in any way that it appears.

Everything in the universe is pure energy, vibrating at different frequencies, including you. There is nothing that rests, even for a second. Everything is in a constant state of motion as it vibrates and travels through time and space. No matter what it is, it is energy and energy is in constant motion. You are energy—your body, your dense vibration which appears physically, is actually just trillions of swiftly moving subatomic particles orbiting each other at a specific vibratory rate. This rate is known as its frequency.

Each thing, every sound, and all of our thoughts, emotions and words have their own unique frequency. Everything that vibrates does so at a certain rate. The higher the frequency, the more potent the force will be. Creative thought is considered the highest form of vibration. Therefore creativity is considered a powerful force in the universe being at this highest frequency.

Imagine the vibrations of your chosen positive thoughts casting out into space, changing things around you as they go. Connect with the power of potentiality as you direct manifestations through the power of creative thought. Anything is possible with a shift in consciousness.

Now, to finish your reading, take three deep cleansing breaths, knowing that with each breath you integrate the information you have received. Trust that this is so, and it will be.

Suggested Applications for Today's Law of Flow

Meditate Use the meditation provided for this Law by finding a quiet place to read the selection, or you can listen to the recording of it (if you have purchased the mp3's that go with this book), or use another meditation that appeals to you. (At least 15 minutes)

Gratitude Write at least three things that you are grateful for on this magnificent day. Connect to the feeling of gratitude.

Exercise Choose an exercise that you feel heightens your vibration.

Hydrate Drink ½ ounce of pure water per pound of body weight (or 30 ml per kg). 2 glasses upon rising, 2 glasses between breakfast and lunch, 2 glasses between lunch and dinner and 2 after dinner.

Life Insight Tune into your imagination and creativity today. What can you create or manifest? Start a creative project that excites you or listen to some inspiring music, anything that will lift your vibration.

Mindful Practice Take a moment, breathe and just be in the present. Become aware of all the movement around you. Notice your body, nature and all around you. Then take that noticing to an internal level. See if you can notice the vibration of your thoughts. If you notice your vibration is not where you want it to be, choose to change it to the vibration that will attract what you are looking for.

Success Strategy First thing in the morning take a moment to visualize your day ahead of you, creating the kind of day you desire mentally and focusing on the successes you will have. Last thing at night, you can use affirmations that will increase your vibration to magnify your success and prepare your subconscious to assimilate and integrate only what you desire while you sleep.

Resources *Edinburgh Lectures on Mental Science* by Thomas Troward
The Dore Lectures on Mental Science by Thomas Troward
The Power of Positive Thinking by Norman Vincent Peale

Day 3: The Law Of Perpetual Transmutation Of Energy

The Law: Energy is in a constant state of transmission and transmutation. Everything vibrates, and it can only change or transform, as it moves from one vibratory rate to another. You can co-create anything.

> *"Change in all things is sweet."*
> Aristotle

My Personal Illustration

Using this Law, I have seen transformations of energy in my various businesses. When I pay attention to the business and increase my energy and get emotionally involved, the sales increase in the business. When I don't infuse energy into the business, the sales start to die off. It is like clockwork: the minute I put energy back into the business, it transmutes into greater sales and increased clients. This Law works in both directions, so as entrepreneurs, it is important to stay energetically involved with a business you want to grow.

Meditation for The Law of Perpetual Transmutation Of Energy

This meditation is a key to unlocking your soul's inner knowing about this Universal Law. It is already in you, so use this time to bring it to your conscious understanding. Read the following meditation slowly.

Take a nice deep breath in through your nose and let it out through your mouth. You are going to let all the tension leave your body, and as you exhale, repeat in your mind the word: Relax.

You are in the right place at the right time. Your body and mind are in a highly creative vibration right now. Your mind and your heart are ready to receive whatever it is that you need to know. You have the best possible guidance to allow you to experience the teachings of this Law, and to gather all the important information in any way that it appears.

Energy is evenly present in all places at all times, but it is in a constant state of transmission and transmutation. Everything vibrates, and it can only change, as it moves from one vibratory rate to another, from a higher frequency to a lower frequency and then back to a higher frequency. All energy is moving into form and out of form and into form and out of form. Energy as a constant vibration is either creating or disintegrating, so nothing ever dies—it only transforms.

You are energy and your brain acts like an electromagnet switching station, which converts light rays into a signal you can understand. Your thoughts are energy that also transform and manifest in your life in direct accordance to your mindset and the type of attention you apply to your thinking. The more attention you give to your idea (especially when you add emotion to it), the faster it can move into form.

By using your mind, you can tap into a higher consciousness and create any image you want and bring it into manifestation into the physical. Everything is here for you to tap into right now. You can co-create anything. You can take a higher vibration and mold it into a denser vibration (a more solid state) in the physical realm. You are a magnificent co-creator.

Now, to finish your reading, take three deep cleansing breaths, knowing that with each breath you integrate the information you have received. Trust that this is so, and it will be.

Suggested Applications for Today's Law of Flow

Meditate Use the meditation provided for this Law by finding a quiet place to read the selection, or you can listen to the recording of it (if you have purchased the mp3's that go with this book), or use another meditation that appeals to you. (At least 15 minutes)

Gratitude Write at least three things that you are grateful for on this magnificent day. Connect to the feeling of gratitude.

Exercise Choose an exercise that you've never done before!

Hydrate Drink ½ ounce of pure water per pound of body weight (or 30 ml per kg). 2 glasses upon rising, 2 glasses between breakfast and lunch, 2 glasses between lunch and dinner and 2 after dinner.

Life Insight Explore what you love to do combined with your talents. You are transforming your passion into action, or transforming your idea into a physical manifestation of it. What would you do for no compensation because you love it? Be a co-creator to bring it to life.

Mindful Practice Take a moment, breathe and just be in the present. Practice using your higher creative faculties to tap into a higher order and create any image you want and bring into manifestation a physical object. If you wish, practice with small ideas first, such as finding a parking space exactly where you want one.

Success Strategy Time your work sessions. Set a timer on your computer or mobile phone. Focus for 90 minutes, then take an active break before setting another 90 minute session. This will keep your energy flowing.

Resources *The Science of Getting Rich* by Wallace D. Wattles
The Magic of Believing by Claude M. Bristol
Think and Grow Rich by Napoleon Hill

Day 4: The Law Of Polarity

The Law: Everything is dual in the physical and mental realms. Even on the quantum level, everything has poles; everything has its pair of opposites. Opposites are identical in nature, but different in degree. This Law provides contrast and clarity: when you know what you don't want, it is easier to determine what you DO want.

> *"The happiness of your life depends*
> *on the quality of your thoughts."*
> Marcus Aurelius Antoninus

My Personal Illustration

This Law has stimulated me to really pursue my inner work. When I figured out that we operate simultaneously on different planes of existence, I quickly realized that my inner work would affect the outer polarity of results. Since my early upbringing was less than exemplary, I had and still have tons of paradigms to tackle. So the inner work was important to achieve the outer results I was looking for. Especially in the area of my vibration, as a child and young adult, I was extremely angry. As I did the work and slowly changed my inner vibration over the years, my outer polarity also changed. More success and peace of mind came my way. Also with the idea of money, when my vibration was one of lack, then the results showed lack. When I changed the polarity to abundance, that opened up the pure potentiality and abundance of the universe.

Meditation for The Law of Polarity

This meditation is a key to unlocking your soul's inner knowing about this Universal Law. It is already in you, so use this time to bring it to your conscious understanding. Read the following meditation slowly.

Take a nice deep breath in through your nose and let it out through your mouth. You are going to let all the tension leave your body, and as you exhale, repeat in your mind the word: Relax.

You are in the right place at the right time. Your body and mind are in a highly creative vibration right now. Your mind and your heart are

ready to receive whatever it is that you need to know. You have the best possible guidance to allow you to experience the teachings of this Law, and to gather all the important information in any way that it appears.

Everything is dual in the physical and mental realms. Even on the quantum level, everything has poles; everything has its pair of opposites. The Law of Polarity states there are two sides to everything. Everything that appears to have an opposite is in fact only two extremes of the same thing. For instance, hot and cold may appear to be opposites, but they are simply varying degrees of the same thing. Opposites are one and the same in nature, but different in vibration. The same applies to positive and negative, good and evil, love and hate, peace and war, light and darkness, energy and matter, waves and particles.

Since everything is vibrating, you can choose to raise your vibration and transform your thoughts from hate to love, from fear to courage. Realize that every condition just is. You make it negative or positive by virtue of how you choose to think about the condition. You can change your perspective and see it from the opposite viewpoint. This Law provides contrast and clarity: when you know what you don't want, it is easier to know what you do want. Make it a habit to focus on the good you want.

Realize that this Law is present with any desire you have. Desire can't exist without the possibility of its fulfillment, even though you can't see it yet.

This principle of duality operates only in the physical and mental realms. Once in the spiritual realm where All is One, there is no possibility for duality. You can access the part of you that is connected to the Universal Mind, behind your thoughts. Allow yourself the quiet space to connect to the Universal Mind and access the consciousness of non-duality.

Now, to finish your reading, take three deep cleansing breaths, knowing that with each breath you integrate the information you have received. Trust that this is so, and it will be.

Suggested Applications for Today's Law of Flow

Meditate Use the meditation provided for this Law by finding a quiet place to read the selection, or you can listen to the recording of it (if you have purchased the mp3's that go with this book), or use another meditation that appeals to you. (At least 15 minutes)

Gratitude Write at least three things that you are grateful for on this magnificent day. Connect to the feeling of gratitude.

Exercise Today, try an exercise that you previously haven't liked very much and find a benefit in it for yourself.

Hydrate Drink ½ ounce of pure water per pound of body weight (or 30 ml per kg). 2 glasses upon rising, 2 glasses between breakfast and lunch, 2 glasses between lunch and dinner and 2 after dinner.

Life Insight Find the good in everything, even events or situations that appear to be the opposite of "good". Reframe your whole day if you have to!

Mindful Practice Take a moment, breathe and just be in the present. When faced with a choice today, close your eyes and place your hand on your heart. As you weigh your options in making your decision, pay attention to how your body feels. By listening to your body, the right answer will reveal itself to you.

Success Strategy Go in the opposite direction of the masses if you want to be successful. Look at the current media to get clues and move in the exact opposite direction. Also look at any challenge you currently are experiencing and look for the polarity of this challenge. Write out three potential obstacles first in the negative. Then replace each negative word with a positive one. Turn around the statements with "I can" and "I will."

Resources *A Treatise on Cosmic Fire* by Alice A. Bailey
Mystic Words of Mighty Power by Walter DeVoe

Day 5: The Law Of Cause And Effect

The Law: In the physical world we live in, every cause has its effect; every effect has its cause. In accordance with this Law, every effect you see in your outside or physical world has a very specific cause, which has its origin in your inner or mental world.

> *"Cause and effect, means and ends, seed and fruit, cannot be severed; for the effect already blooms in the cause, the end preexists in the means, the fruit in the seed."*
> Ralph Waldo Emerson

My Personal Illustration

I have always believed that one person's actions can change the world for good. When I began to care for my personal environment, the results were dramatic. I had some re-occurring allergies and rashes before I changed my cleaning products to non-toxic ones and after a month or so of using the safe Get Clean products, my symptoms disappeared. It turned out that the **cause** of the allergies and rashes were the regular cleaners I had been using, and when I switched over to non-toxic, the **effect** was a new result. It didn't take long before I began sharing my results with others and expanding my reach, starting environmental campaigns to help clean up our waterways.

"Treat the earth well: it was not given to you by your parents, it was loaned to you by your children. We do not inherit the Earth from our Ancestors, we borrow it from our Children" is an ancient Indian proverb. This quote reminds me to keep my focus on the goal of having an environmentally-sustainable world, and that through the use of this law we can be the cause for healthy effects for the planet.

Meditation for The Law of Cause and Effect

This meditation is a key to unlocking your soul's inner knowing about this Universal Law. It is already in you, so use this time to bring it to your conscious understanding. Read the following meditation slowly.

Take a nice deep breath in through your nose and let it out through your mouth. You are going to let all the tension leave your body, and as you exhale, repeat in your mind the word: Relax.

You are in the right place at the right time. Your body and mind are in a highly creative vibration right now. Your mind and your heart are ready to receive whatever it is that you need to know. You have the best possible guidance to allow you to experience the teachings of this Law, and to gather all the important information in any way that it appears.

In the physical world we live in, every cause has its effect; every effect has its cause. For every action, there is an equal and opposite reaction. In accordance with this Law, every effect you see in your outside or physical world has a very specific cause, which originates from your inner or mental thought world. When you come to understand that everything in your reality is a mental creation, you appreciate the importance of mastering your mind. You are always at cause. You reap what you sow. Your current results are the effect of your past thinking and your behavior. This is the essence of thought power. Every one of your thoughts sets a specific effect in motion, which will materialize over time as a result. Every action has a reaction and consequence. Some call this the Law of Karma.

The Law of Cause and Effect applies on all planes of existence. We notice this Law because our concept of time and space creates a time lag between the cause and the eventual effect.

Be aware that what you'd like to create in the physical world exists first in the non-material world, and with continued concentrated thought, perseverance and emotional desire, it will become visible in your physical world. Where there is a cause, there is an effect. Nothing ever happens by chance. Your job is to create the causes on the mental plane that are consistent with the effects that you want to enjoy in your life. The Law of Attraction will aid you in your creation.

Feel the pure potential of your creative thought vibration as it aligns with the power that manifests everything in the universe.

Now, to finish your reading, take three deep cleansing breaths, knowing that with each breath you integrate the information you have received. Trust that this is so, and it will be.

Suggested Applications for Today's Law of Flow

Meditate Use the meditation provided for this Law by finding a quiet place to read the selection, or you can listen to the recording of it (if you have purchased the mp3's that go with this book), or use another meditation that appeals to you. (At least 15 minutes)

Gratitude Write at least three things that you are grateful for on this magnificent day. Connect to the feeling of gratitude.

Exercise Notice what changes have already taken place in your body over the last five days of exercising. And make sure to exercise today too!

Hydrate Drink ½ ounce of pure water per pound of body weight (or 30 ml per kg). 2 glasses upon rising, 2 glasses between breakfast and lunch, 2 glasses between lunch and dinner and 2 after dinner.

Life Insight Understand how you've created your world, with actions of your body, speech and mind. It is incredibly empowering to know that your future is in your hands. Look at what you have created. If you're not happy with it, change one habit that will lead to what you want to create.

Mindful Practice Take a moment, breathe and just be in the present. Take a moment today to listen to a common message you send your body. Is it a message of kindness, respect, and love? If not, rephrase what you are telling your body and repeat that new message often throughout the day.

Success Strategy Contemplate which thoughts, beliefs, perceptions, assumptions, scripts, values, emotions, or behaviors caused an effect or result that you were not in pleased with. What needs to change in order to get a different result? Look around for successful people you can model. How can you model their winning behaviors, habits, decisions and actions?

Resources *Science of Being in Twenty Seven Lessons* by Eugene A. Fersen *The Science of Mind* by Ernest Holmes

Day 6: The Law Of Rhythm

The Law: The Law of Rhythm explains how everything in the universe has its own rhythm. These rhythms are what the cycle of life is all about. There is always a reaction to every action. It is important to realize which season you are experiencing in your life.

> *"Everything flows, out and in; everything has its tides; all things rise and fall; the pendulum-swing manifests in every- thing; the measure of the swing to the right is the measure of the swing to the left; rhythm compensates."*
> The Kybalion

My Personal Illustration

Biorhythm devices measure our cycles (physical, emotional, and intellec- tual cycles). Many people report that they can improve their quality of life by monitoring the highs and lows of these cycles and acting accordingly.

I prefer to use my own inner compass with this Law, and do so every time I'm not feeling well. Using the concept of subtle impermanence (a Buddhist term), I know that my body will swing back into health again. This Law keeps me going when I am down, knowing that I will be back on an upward swing soon. The only time I "milk" the illness is when I need an excuse to rest. That's when I may elongate the process to take a little more time off and have an "excuse" to rest a little longer!

In business, I have had cycles of lean times and then the pendulum swings to abundance. Using this Law, I know not to focus on the lean times since that will prolong the cycle. Relax in knowing that everything is constantly moving and that the cycle will rebound if you stay conscious of these Laws and focus on your desires.

Meditation for The Law of Rhythm

This meditation is a key to unlocking your soul's inner knowing about this Universal Law. It is already in you, so use this time to bring it to your conscious understanding. Read the following meditation slowly.

Take a nice deep breath in through your nose and let it out through your mouth. You are going to let all the tension leave your body, and as you exhale, repeat in your mind the word: Relax.

You are in the right place at the right time. Your body and mind are in a highly creative vibration right now. Your mind and your heart are ready to receive whatever it is that you need to know. You have the best possible guidance to allow you to experience the teachings of this Law, and to gather all the important information in any way that it appears.

The Law of Rhythm explains how everything in the universe has its own rhythm. These rhythms are what create the seasons. These rhythms are what the cycle of life is all about. There is always a reaction to every action. This is the Law of Attraction in action. Everything flows, out and in; everything has its tides; all things rise and fall; the pendulum-swing manifests in everything; the measure of the swing to the right is the measure of the swing to the left; rhythm compensates.

Rhythm can be seen in the waves of the ocean, in business cycles, stages of your development, in the swinging of your thoughts from being negative to positive and in your personal failures and successes.

It is important to realize which season you are experiencing in your life. Are you in the season to sow seeds, or are you in the harvest, reaping the rewards of your labor? Are you in the winter, summer, spring or fall? You can't ignore these rhythms. You may notice you can feel differently from day to day as well. Some days you are "up" and some days you are "down". With your understanding of this Law and your free will, you can create the right attitude to weather the season you are experiencing. Even when the energy is on a downswing, find comfort that by virtue of this very same Law, the upward motion must swing back again.

The meaning you give any of the events in your life will determine how you think and feel about them, which in turn creates another rhythm within you. Determine whether you were the cause of a downward swing or if it was just the natural rhythm. All cycles have seasons to them and with this knowledge you can plan ahead to prepare for the next cycle. You can choose thoughts that will help you get through the rhythm more naturally. Go with the flow. If you are in winter right now, start planning for spring and for summer, as the thoughts you have today will set up the rhythm of where you are going.

You can choose to see the positive aspect of every season and harvest the best of what that season offers. Be cradled in the rhythm of the universe.

Now, to finish your reading, take three deep cleansing breaths, knowing that with each breath you integrate the information you have received. Trust that this is so, and it will be.

Suggested Applications for Today's Law of Flow

Meditate Use the meditation provided for this Law by finding a quiet place to read the selection, or you can listen to the recording of it (if you have purchased the mp3's that go with this book), or use another meditation that appeals to you. (At least 15 minutes)

Gratitude Write at least three things that you are grateful for on this magnificent day. Connect to the feeling of gratitude.

Exercise Add music to your exercise today.

Hydrate Drink ½ ounce of pure water per pound of body weight (or 30 ml per kg). 2 glasses upon rising, 2 glasses between breakfast and lunch, 2 glasses between lunch and dinner and 2 after dinner.

Life Insight Pay attention to the rhythms occurring in your life right now. Go for a walk and notice with all your senses the places that express rhythm in your world.

Mindful Practice Take a moment, breathe and just be in the present. Spend some time practicing conscious breathing. Get comfortable and close your eyes. Begin to notice the breath as it flows in and out of the nostrils. After a few rounds of inhalations and exhalations, notice the rhythm of your breathing.

Success Strategy Make time to rest your body and mind. That's the only way to stay energized and create success. Take active breaks to keep your energy flowing. Create balance in your life. Don't wait for someone to design it for you, only you can intend it for yourself. Establish a rhythm by scheduling money-making days, buffer days and free days. Wake up the same time every day. Start each day with a healthy Shaklee protein Smoothee mixed with water and greens.

Resources *Book of the Law* by Aleister Crowley
Fractal Time by Gregg Braden

Day 7: The Law Of Relativity

The Law: Nothing is big or small, good or bad, unless you relate it to something else. It just is. It is your judgment and perception combined that make things look the way they do including your reality.

> *"Nothing is either good or bad, but your*
> *thinking makes it so."*
> William Shakespeare in *Hamlet*

My Personal Illustration

The best illustration of this Law comes with the story of the Taoist Farmer. It is not my personal illustration this time but it was too good not to include here:

A farmer had only one horse, and one day the horse ran away. The neighbors came to condole over his terrible loss. The farmer said, "What makes you think it is so terrible?"

A month later, the horse came home–this time bringing with her two beautiful wild horses. The neighbors became excited at the farmer's good fortune. Such lovely strong horses! The farmer said, "What makes you think this is good fortune?"

The farmer's son was thrown from one of the wild horses and broke his leg. All the neighbors were very distressed. Such bad luck! The farmer said, "What makes you think it is bad?"

A war came, and every able-bodied man was conscripted and sent into battle. Only the farmer's son, because he had a broken leg, remained. The neighbors congratulated the farmer. "What makes you think this is good?" said the farmer.

I think you get the idea with this story. Nothing is good or bad unless you relate it to something else. It just IS.

So too in our business or our personal life: if things appear to not be going well, use this Law and see any event through this perception: nothing has meaning but for the meaning we give it.

Meditation for the Law of Relativity

This meditation is a key to unlocking your soul's inner knowing about this Universal Law. It is already in you, so use this time to bring it to your conscious understanding. Read the following meditation slowly.

Take a nice deep breath in through your nose and let it out through your mouth. You are going to let all the tension leave your body, and as you exhale, repeat in your mind the word: Relax.

You are in the right place at the right time. Your body and mind are in a highly creative vibration right now. Your mind and your heart are ready to receive whatever it is that you need to know. You have the best possible guidance to allow you to experience the teachings of this Law, and to gather all the important information in any way that it appears.

The Law of Relativity states that all things are relative, even the other Laws. Nothing is good or bad, big or small unless you relate it to something else. It just IS. It is your judgment and perception that make things look good or bad, big or small and so on.

When you look at and face your own personal challenges, you can see that there is always someone on a journey facing and surmounting their own possibly even more difficult situations. We are all given challenges for a reason, as opportunities to learn and grow. This comparison could offer you the feeling of tapping into the Law of Gratitude.

Comparing yourself negatively to other people's circumstances is a waste, because their situations are different. Always focus on what you want without comparing it and then you won't fall into the trap of self-judging and using this Law against yourself.

Begin using this Law to realize that it is your perception that creates your reality. Become aware of how special and unique you are. Be gentle with yourself and relax into all that is.

Now, to finish your reading, take three deep cleansing breaths, knowing that with each breath you integrate the information you have received. Trust that this is so, and it will be.

Suggested Applications for Today's Law of Flow

Meditate Use the meditation provided for this Law by finding a quiet place to read the selection, or you can listen to the recording of it (if you have purchased the mp3's that go with this book), or use another meditation that appeals to you. (At least 15 minutes)

Gratitude Write at least three things that you are grateful for on this magnificent day. Connect to the feeling of gratitude.

Exercise Choose an exercise you can do with another person and see what that brings to your quality of exercise.

Hydrate Drink ½ ounce of pure water per pound of body weight (or 30 ml per kg). 2 glasses upon rising, 2 glasses between breakfast and lunch, 2 glasses between lunch and dinner and 2 after dinner.

Life Insight Spend some time with a group of friends or colleagues. Notice the uniqueness of each individual and how your perception about them is relative to another person or idea.

Mindful Practice Take a moment, breathe and just be in the present. Notice how your judgment and perception make things appear one way or another, at one extreme or another. Could you see something differently by changing your evaluation of it, or by taking it away completely—by making it neither good nor bad?

Success Strategy Think of three obstacles that you can turn into advantages. Consider looking at them from another perspective. See if they are really true. Do research if necessary. Ask for other opinions.

Resources *The Light Shall Set You Free* by Norma Manalovitch
The Quantum World by Kenneth W. Ford

Day 8: The Law Of Gender

The Law: Gender is in everything; everything has its masculine and feminine principles, and this is where creation begins. This Law also decrees that every seed has a gestation or incubation time. Ideas are spiritual seeds and can move into physical results.

> *"The universal order and the personal order are nothing but different expressions and manifestations of a common underlying principle."*
> Marcus Aurelius

My Personal Illustration

When I wrote my first book, I gave it a deadline. I wanted it to be done for my birthday. So I set about writing it and within a few months of my deadline, I began to work with the editors and the typesetters and search for the right printer. I was not in tune with the Universal Laws at that time in my life, so as my deadline approached, I started to push the envelope a little, not realizing the Law of Gender. The bottom line was that my book did not get published when I wanted it, but in terms of the Universal Law, it was as it was supposed to be.

With another book I co-wrote, we finished the book at a time when a whole new audience appeared that we did not know about as we were writing the book. So on the unseen level, we were creating a book that would support an audience that was searching for exactly what we had published. The gestation time was perfect for the manifestation of that book.

With any business be aware of this Law and be gentle with yourself if your timelines don't always work out. A more profound timeline may be at work.

Meditation for The Law of Gender

This meditation is a key to unlocking your soul's inner knowing about this Universal Law. It is already in you, so use this time to bring it to your conscious understanding. Read the following meditation slowly.

Take a nice deep breath in through your nose and let it out through your mouth. You are going to let all the tension leave your body, and as you exhale, repeat in your mind the word: Relax.

You are in the right place at the right time. Your body and mind are in a highly creative vibration right now. Your mind and your heart are ready to receive whatever it is that you need to know. You have the best possible guidance to allow you to experience the teachings of this Law, and to gather all the important information in any way that it appears.

The Law of Gender is evident throughout creation. Gender is in everything; everything has its masculine and feminine principles. Everything from plants, minerals, electrons, to humans contains both the masculine and feminine elements, and this is how creation takes place in the universe.

Open yourself to these gender principles to create balance in your life. As a spiritual being, you must balance the masculine and feminine energies (the Yin and Yang) within yourself to become a true co-creator with the Universal Consciousness. When you know this, you will know what it means to be whole and complete.

This Law also declares that every seed has a gestation or incubation period. Ideas are spiritual seeds and can move into physical results. Perhaps you might know the gestation time of a carrot seed, or of a baby, but you don't always know the gestation time of an idea. Understanding this Law will help you appreciate that patience is sometimes required on the physical plane, as you don't always see the materialization when you desire it. It varies on the amount of focus, feeling, expectation, gratitude and stabilization of frequency you are able to bring to your manifestation. Trust in the Universal Intelligence to determine the time in which it will take for the manifestation or the physical representation of that thought or idea. Here is where trust and belief are required so you don't get in your own way and mess up the process.

Be clear on your seed, be patient, feel the gratefulness, focus on your vibration and watch the magic of creation.

Now, to finish your reading, take three deep cleansing breaths, knowing that with each breath you integrate the information you have received. Trust that this is so, and it will be.

Suggested Applications for Today's Law of Flow

Meditate Use the meditation provided for this Law by finding a quiet place to read the selection, or you can listen to the recording of it (if you have purchased the mp3's that go with this book), or use another meditation that appeals to you. (At least 15 minutes)

Gratitude Write at least three things that you are grateful for on this magnificent day. Connect to the feeling of gratitude.

Exercise Choose a longer time to exercise today to see what difference it can make.

Hydrate Drink ½ ounce of pure water per pound of body weight (or 30 ml per kg). 2 glasses upon rising, 2 glasses between breakfast and lunch, 2 glasses between lunch and dinner and 2 after dinner.

Life Insight Set a timeline for an action step towards one of your goals, keep the vision of your goal but don't get too attached to the date. Expect that this Law will work with you to manifest that action at the perfect time for its coming into being.

Mindful Practice Take a moment, breathe and just be in the present. Contemplate Carl Sagan's quote, "The absence of evidence is not evidence of absence." Or Price Pritchett's version, "Absence of evidence does not mean evidence of absence."

Success Strategy Meditate or contemplate the quote by Saint Augustine. "Faith is to believe what you do not see; the reward of this faith is to see what you believe." Connect with nature on your breaks.

Resources *The Law and the Word* by Thomas Troward
How To Use Your Power by Ernest Holmes

Day 9: The Law Of Oneness and Pure Potentiality

The Law: The Law of Oneness explains how you relate to the All; everything is intertwined. The nature of the Universal Mind is all-knowing, all-powerful, all-creative and always present. Your mind is part of this one Universal Mind and since your thoughts are a product of your mind, it follows that your thought power too is limitless and full of pure potentiality.

> *"All differences in this world are of degree, and not of kind,*
> *because oneness is the secret of everything."*
> Swami Vivekananda

My Personal Illustration
This Law feels like the most important one of all for me.

As a young child, I used to talk to angels and God all the time, so I had a sense of being connected to something beyond what I could see. But this wasn't nearly as powerful as the "direct experience" I had years later as adult. (Note: I always find it hard to describe this experience as words don't do it justice.)

I was in a beautiful park on a gorgeous day. The sun was shining, the birds chirping, and I walked onto a bridge with a beautiful little creek flowing underneath it and paused. As I listened to the gurgle of the water and took in all that nature was providing, all of a sudden I was totally connected with the All. "I" disappeared and became one with everything. My consciousness united with the All-ness of Everything and everything became one. There was nothing separate from me, and yet there was a sense of me being in everything.

It was a life-changing experience; my previous beliefs around religion evaporated in a second, and I've seen the world from a totally different perspective ever since. I am so grateful to have had this experience, because now I know that this state exists, no matter how separate I may feel from it day to day.

From a business point of view, when we are in the flow we are connected with the abundance of the universe and anything is possible. When we aim for this vibration, then our co-creation is immeasurable and anything is possible. The 30 Day Plan is geared to raise our vibration to this level.

Meditation for The Law Of Oneness and Pure Potentiality

This meditation is a key to unlocking your soul's inner knowing about this Universal Law. It is already in you, so use this time to bring it to your conscious understanding. Read the following meditation slowly.

Take a nice deep breath in through your nose and let it out through your mouth. You are going to let all the tension leave your body, and as you exhale, repeat in your mind the word: Relax.

You are in the right place at the right time. Your body and mind are in a highly creative vibration right now. Your mind and your heart are ready to receive whatever it is that you need to know. You have the best possible guidance to allow you to experience the teachings of this Law, and to gather all the important information in any way that it appears.

The Law of Oneness says there is a single, intelligent Universal Consciousness—the Universal Mind—from which all aspects of consciousness manifest. It permeates the entire universe, and is present everywhere at the same time as pure potentiality.

Everything you see and experience in your physical world has its origin in the invisible, mental realm. Everything, at its core, consists of pure energy and everything is interconnected with everything else, both the visible (on the physical) and the invisible (on the metaphysical). Think of all things, including yourself, as a vibrating mass of pure energy that is interconnected to everything else. You really are part of the one. Everything you do, say, think or believe is connected and influences all others in this vast universe.

To put it another way, anything and everything which exists in the entire cosmos, when broken down and analyzed into its most basic form with sophisticated scientific tools and instruments, is shown to be a vibrating frequency of energy. This energy is a unified field of intelligence, a field of consciousness, pure potentiality. It joins together with energies of the same harmonious frequency to form what you perceive (and as a result, experience), in the physical world.

The Universal Mind goes by many names. In the scientific world we know of the Unified Field. In spiritual philosophy we refer to it as The All, The Law, All-Knowing Great Spirit, Divine Intelligence, Source Energy, The I Am That I Am, Universal Consciousness, or Universal Intelligence. In religion, we call upon God who Himself goes by many names: the Creator, the Source, Divine Mind, Love, Father, Goddess, Great Spirit, Gitche Manitou, Jehovah, Lord, Tao, Allah and Brahma, to mention but a few.

Consciousness itself is the foundation of all known forces and energies in creation. Consciousness is Life! Know that this too is your nature. Your mind is part of this one Universal Mind and since your thoughts are a product of your mind, it follows that your thought power is limitless, full of pure potentiality too. You have access to all knowledge, the known and the unknown. You have access to the limitless creativity and pure potentiality of the Universal Mind. You have access to this infinite power for which nothing is impossible. All these attributes are present within you at all times in their potential form. Connecting here is the ultimate Mastermind.

The reality you create is a manifestation of your mind. Once you truly understand that your mind is one with the Universal Mind, you can create the reality of your choice as you are in touch with pure potentiality.

Nothing and no one is separate from you. The sense of separation you experience in the physical world is created by the way your five senses interpret this infinite ocean of vibrating energy. You are one with the One Universal Mind from which all things become manifest. And we are all connected.

Now, to finish your reading, take three deep cleansing breaths, knowing that with each breath you integrate the information you have received. Trust that this is so, and it will be.

Suggested Applications for Today's Law of Flow

Meditate Use the meditation provided for this Law by finding a quiet place to read the selection, or you can listen to the recording of it (if you have purchased the mp3's that go with this book), or use another meditation that appeals to you. (At least 15 minutes)

Gratitude Write at least three things that you are grateful for on this magnificent day. Connect to the feeling of gratitude.

Exercise Go outside for your exercise today and see how connected you feel with your surroundings even while exercising.

Hydrate Drink ½ ounce of pure water per pound of body weight (or 30 ml per kg). 2 glasses upon rising, 2 glasses between breakfast and lunch, 2 glasses between lunch and dinner and 2 after dinner.

Life Insight Develop your surrendering. Allow yourself to tap into Universal Intelligence—it knows what you want, let the Universal Intelligence guide you today. Look around you today and let nature be your role model. Go within and feel the connection.

Mindful Practice Take a moment, breathe and just be in the present. Find a sheet of paper and divide it in half with a line down the middle. In the left column write the word "Self". In the right column write "Universe". Write out what you intend to accomplish today in the side marked "Self". Then write what you want to delegate to the Universe to handle. Now comes the important part: release the side that you want the Universe to handle. Completely let it go. You are now free to really focus on what you intend to do.

Success Strategy Follow your intuition. Your gut feeling is more often right than not. You may not understand it now but you might understand it in hindsight.

Resources *The Law of Thinking* from Raymond Holliwell's *Working With The Law*

Illusions by Richard Bach

Stillness Speaks by Eckhart Tolle

In Tune with the Infinite by Ralph Waldo Trine

Taking the Quantum Leap: The New Physics for Nonscientists by Fred A. Wolf

Entanglement by Gregg Braden

Day 10: The Law Of Supply and Abundance

The Law: Basically the Law of Supply boils down to the belief in abundance. You live in a universe of abundance. The universe will never run out of anything you desire and there is enough for everyone. It will always supply you with what you want, when you want it. You just have to ask.

"There is a supply for every demand."
Florence Scovel Shinn

My Personal Illustration

I learned in my early twenties that when I decided I wanted something, I would get it. Once I made the decision, the Law of Supply and Abundance worked on my behalf. Once, I made the decision to go away on a personal development program, but I did not have the money for the trip. I simply made the decision to go and kept seeing myself there. Just in time, some work I wasn't expecting came my way and it was enough to pay for everything I needed. So sometimes we are just a decision away from all the supply that exists around us.

A simple example is my vegetable garden. Each year I watch this Law at work. I am in awe of all the abundance that nature provides, even without my constant and direct attention.

Meditation for The Law Of Supply and Abundance

This meditation is a key to unlocking your soul's inner knowing about this Universal Law. It is already in you, so use this time to bring it to your conscious understanding. Read the following meditation slowly.

Take a nice deep breath in through your nose and let it out through your mouth. You are going to let all the tension leave your body, and as you exhale, repeat in your mind the word: Relax.

You are in the right place at the right time. Your body and mind are in a highly creative vibration right now. Your mind and your heart are ready to receive whatever it is that you need to know. You have the best possible guidance to allow you to experience the teachings of this Law, and to gather all the important information in any way that it appears.

You live in a universe of abundance. It is endless; it will never run out of anything you desire and there is enough for everyone. It will always supply you with what you want, when you want it. You just have to ask, and allow, without getting in the way. You have within yourself everything required to make your earthly incarnation a paradise if you choose to accept that which is your divine birthright. Basically the Law of Supply boils down to the belief in abundance.

Masters throughout time have told us that when we align with Divine Consciousness, we are able to continually manifest both internal abundance and the material expression of that abundance. They have also said that abundance is not something that is reserved for a special few, though it might often seem that way. All that is required is a change of awareness in consciousness.

The Law of Supply and Abundance allows you to evolve, to create, to accomplish, to move forward; in other words to succeed. This spiritual Law of Supply and Abundance is based on the concept that everything you need is already available to you; all you need to do is be open to it the vibration of it.

Just observe nature and you will see the Law of Supply and Abundance working all the time. Simply know that abundance is all around you, align yourself with it by practicing the other Laws of Flow, and watch how abundance shows up for you.

Now, to finish your reading, take three deep cleansing breaths, knowing that with each breath you integrate the information you have received. Trust that this is so, and it will be.

Suggested Applications for Today's Law of Flow

Meditate Use the meditation provided for this Law by finding a quiet place to read the selection, or you can listen to the recording of it (if you have purchased the mp3's that go with this book), or use another meditation that appeals to you. (At least 15 minutes)

Gratitude Write at least three things that you are grateful for on this magnificent day. Connect to the feeling of gratitude.

Exercise Be aware of the abundance of oxygen around you. Connect to your breath as you are exercising, because that never runs out until you take your last one!

Hydrate Drink ½ ounce of pure water per pound of body weight (or 30 ml per kg). 2 glasses upon rising, 2 glasses between breakfast and lunch, 2 glasses between lunch and dinner and 2 after dinner.

Life Insight Make a commitment to keep wealth circulating in your life by giving and receiving life's most precious gifts: the gifts of caring, understanding, affection, appreciation, and love. With each encounter today, silently wish each person happiness, health, love and laughter.

Mindful Practice Take a moment, breathe and just be in the present. Commit to spending some time in nature today. Whether you choose to be active or simply take in the bounty around you, express your heartfelt gratitude for all that nature offers you and for your place in this beautiful planet.

Success Strategy Read *Chapter 3: Is Opportunity Monopolized?* from *The Science of Getting Rich* by Wallace D. Wattles. (If you feel you really want to study this chapter in greater depth, then find a buddy and read it aloud for 30 days. If you miss a day, then start all over again until you do 30 days in a row.)

Resources *The Power of Now: A Guide to Spiritual Enlightenment* by Eckhart Tolle

The Field: The Quest for the Secret Force of the Universe by Lynne McTaggart

The Law of Supply from Raymond Holliwell's *Working With The Law*

Day 11: The Law Of Correspondence

The Law: This Law tells us as above, so below; as below, so above, everything has its own corresponding counterpart. Everything on the physical plane has a corresponding principle out there in the universe.

"Just as a knowledge of the Principles of Geometry enables man to measure distant suns and their movements while seated in his observatory, so a knowledge of the Principle of Correspondence enables Man to reason intelligently from the Known to the Unknown."
The Kybalion

My Personal Illustration

Every time I change my inner thinking about something, it shows up in my outer reality. Sometimes that means letting go of an old paradigm or habit that is not serving me anymore and sometimes it means taking on a new belief.

For example, when I started my first book I had to let go of an old paradigm that I was not a good writer. When I changed my thinking, I produced a bestselling book.

After college, I had the belief that school was over for me for the rest of my life. In my early thirties, I changed that belief and enrolled in a full-time program and even though I was the oldest student by far, it didn't distract me from my goal to become a Drugless Practitioner. This experience led me to even more schooling and today I am so grateful that I changed that belief system, as higher education has opened many doors for me as an entrepreneur.

If you want to be really successful in business, pay attention to your inner world as your outer world corresponds to it.

Meditation for The Law of Correspondence

This meditation is a key to unlocking your soul's inner knowing about this Universal Law. It is already in you, so use this time to bring it to your conscious understanding. Read the following meditation slowly.

Take a nice deep breath in through your nose and let it out through your mouth. You are going to let all the tension leave your body, and as you exhale, repeat in your mind the word: Relax.

You are in the right place at the right time. Your body and mind are in a highly creative vibration right now. Your mind and your heart are ready to receive whatever it is that you need to know. You have the best possible guidance to allow you to experience the teachings of this Law, and to gather all the important information in any way that it appears.

The Law of Correspondence explains the Law of Attraction. This Universal Law tells us "As Above, So Below": everything has its own corresponding counterpart. The same pattern is expressed on all planes of existence from the smallest electron to the largest star and vice versa.

In the same way, the outer world is nothing more than a reflection of the inner world—so you could also say: as without, so within. Your current reality is a mirror of what is going on inside you. This Law says that if your inner world contains very noble, worthy values and qualities that you adhere to and refuse to compromise, your outer world will correspond to those values and qualities.

If you desire change in your outer world, you must first change your inner world—your thoughts, beliefs, assumptions and attitudes. Your current situation is a direct result of your past thoughts.

The inscription on the Ancient Greek Temple of Apollo at Delphi "Know thyself and thou shalt know all the mysteries of the gods and the universe" sums up this Law quite nicely. Imagine the connection of macrocosm to microcosm and vice versa, from grains of sand to stars in the sky.

Now, to finish your reading, take three deep cleansing breaths, knowing that with each breath you integrate the information you have received. Trust that this is so, and it will be.

Suggested Applications for Today's Law of Flow

Meditate Use the meditation provided for this Law by finding a quiet place to read the selection, or you can listen to the recording of it (if you have purchased the mp3's that go with this book), or use another meditation that appeals to you. (At least 15 minutes)

Gratitude Write at least three things that you are grateful for on this magnificent day. Connect to the feeling of gratitude.

Exercise Hold the image of your ideal body proportions as you exercise. Imagine in great detail your strength level, endurance, balance, and grace.

Hydrate Drink ½ ounce of pure water per pound of body weight (or 30 ml per kg). 2 glasses upon rising, 2 glasses between breakfast and lunch, 2 glasses between lunch and dinner and 2 after dinner.

Life Insight Be aware that conformity is the opposite of courage. When we don't confront the conventional way, it is harder to hear our own desires. Take some time to examine your environment and consider those things you'd like to change. Remind yourself that your outer world is a reflection of your inner world; have the courage to explore what you really want and be a non-conformist.

Mindful Practice Take a moment, breathe and just be in the present. Be mindful that without self-awareness, you are at the mercy of your patterns, old habits, assumptions, paradigms or conditioning. Of what thought or belief are you ready to let go? What thought or belief are you ready to adopt? Be conscious of what you really yearn for today.

Success Strategy Look at your patterns, old habits, values, assumptions, paradigms or conditioning around your business. What is not serving you any longer? What thought or belief are you ready to adopt that would lead you to more success? Or what new habit do you want to adopt?

Resources *Power of Intention* by Dr. Wayne Dyer

As A Man Thinketh by James Allen

Day 12: The Law Of Attraction

The Law: All of your thoughts, feelings, words and actions produce energy, which in turn attracts like energies and things into your life. You attract into your life those things, circumstances, and conditions that correspond with the nature of your dominant habitual vibration, contributed to by your thoughts, expectations and beliefs, both conscious and subconscious. Remember: Everything vibrates. It really is important to realize that the shift must be with your energetic vibration; changing your thoughts alone is not enough.

> *"We're all working with one power, one law. It's Attraction."*
> Bob Proctor

My Personal Illustration

This is a fun Law to work with. When I was single and wanted to attract a partner, I would sit down with girlfriends and come up with a list describing the perfect man. At the time I did not understand that I was attracting a mirror of who I was being at that time. But for every instance that I actually took the time to write out a description, the universe would provide an exact match to my desires. As time progressed, my list would become more specific as sometimes my partners would show me what I didn't want. As I changed, my list of attributes changed as well.

In business, the base of this Law of Attraction (the Law of Vibration) is very important. Over the years, whatever I was vibrating is what I attracted. As I modified my vibration, I began to attract different types of people into my businesses. We attract who we are. (You will see this later in the Law of Reflection.)

Meditation for The Law of Attraction

This meditation is a key to unlocking your soul's inner knowing about this Universal Law. It is already in you, so use this time to bring it to your conscious understanding. Read the following meditation slowly.

Take a nice deep breath in through your nose and let it out through your mouth. You are going to let all the tension leave your body, and as you exhale, repeat in your mind the word: Relax.

You are in the right place at the right time. Your body and mind are in a highly creative vibration right now. Your mind and your heart are ready to receive whatever it is that you need to know. You have the best possible guidance to allow you to experience the teachings of this Law, and to gather all the important information in any way that it appears.

To understand the Law of Attraction correctly, you must remember the Law of Vibration (Day 2). The two go hand in hand. There is no separation of the two. When you apply one, you also apply the other. Remember your thoughts are vibrations; waves of energy that penetrate all time and space. When you think of something, and vibrate with it, you are creating a frequency. That frequency goes out into the universe and reaches an item that also vibrates at that same frequency. When this happens, the two are in harmony. The electromagnetic waves that your brain creates from your thoughts vibrate to the exact energy level as the thing or item in the universe for which you have asked (either consciously or unconsciously). By concentrating on these specific, focused thought patterns, you increase the energy level of those thoughts and so the thoughts become more potent. Your thoughts transform the invisible to the visible.

In accordance with this Law, you attract into your life those things, circumstances and conditions that correspond with the nature of your dominant, habitual thoughts, expectations and beliefs, both conscious and subconscious. Your habitual thoughts, beliefs and your dominant mental attitude determine your dominant frequency. When you consistently maintain a positive mental attitude, you attract positive experiences and circumstances while a predominantly negative mental attitude attracts those conditions deemed negative or unwanted.

You cannot attract that which you do not radiate. What you focus on will be attracted to you. Feel yourself vibrating in the positive energy of love, acceptance, and more joy in living and watch how you attract it to you in a myriad of ways.

Now, to finish your reading, take three deep cleansing breaths, knowing that with each breath you integrate the information you have received. Trust that this is so, and it will be.

Suggested Applications for Today's Law of Flow

Meditate Use the meditation provided for this Law by finding a quiet place to read the selection, or you can listen to the recording of it (if you have purchased the mp3's that go with this book), or use another meditation that appeals to you. (At least 15 minutes)

Gratitude Write at least three things that you are grateful for on this magnificent day. Connect to the feeling of gratitude.

Exercise As you exercise state this affirmation: "I am in the process of becoming truly healthy and enjoying every minute of my exercise."

Hydrate Drink ½ ounce of pure water per pound of body weight (or 30 ml per kg). 2 glasses upon rising, 2 glasses between breakfast and lunch, 2 glasses between lunch and dinner and 2 after dinner.

Life Insight Find an attractive box that you like. Gather pictures from magazines or items that express your current desire, something you want to attract to you. You can also include written descriptions of your desire. Then on the outside of the box, write: "Whatever is contained in this box IS".

Mindful Practice Take a moment, breathe and just be in the present. Practice some affirmations. "I choose to create this or something better." "I am in the process of becoming...." You fill in the blank. Repeat these affirmations daily to create a new belief of what you want to attract.

Success Strategy Stay positive. Your mindset controls your happiness so take care to control your mindset. Feeling low? Smile. Simple changes in your body language can improve how you're feeling as well as spread good vibes around you. Create a pleasing personality that attracts others to you.

Resources *The Secret* by Rhonda Byrne

Ask & It Is Given: Learning to Manifest Your Desires by Esther Hicks

The Law of Attraction from Raymond Holliwell's *Working With The Law*

Day 13: The Law Of Increase

The Law: Whenever you utilize the Law of Increase, you raise your consciousness toward a higher realm. Giving praise or being grateful is one of the most powerful ways to speed up the delivery of the things you want to manifest. I like to think of praise and gratitude as faith in action.

"Giving opens the way for receiving."
Florence Scovel Shinn

My Personal Illustration

As a teenager, I was very fortunate to have a teacher take me under her wing and praise me for my gymnastic and dance ability. This led to increased confidence in this area and I pursued dance with a passion from that point on.

Working with this Law, increased my vibration. At times over the years I felt that I wanted to give complimentary sessions in my business. Each time I gave something away, I felt the increase and the receiver felt very grateful for the gift.

I also taught clients a little song, "Every little cell in my body is healthy, every little cell in my body is well. The tune is the same as Mama's Little Baby Loves Shortnin' Bread. This affirmation focused on praise for our cells.

I also have been very fortunate to be able to share my abundance with four foster children around the world. The increased vibration is so wonderful especially when I receive letters back to hear how my support is helping them with schooling and other essentials of life.

As an entrepreneur I support other fledgling entrepreneurs through offering seed capital for their businesses through an organization called Kiva. This sends the message of increase to those entrepreneurs, applauds their efforts and gives them the opportunity to pursue their dreams.

Meditation for The Law Of Increase

This meditation is a key to unlocking your soul's inner knowing about this Universal Law. It is already in you, so use this time to bring it to your conscious understanding. Read the following meditation slowly.

Take a nice deep breath in through your nose and let it out through your mouth. You are going to let all the tension leave your body, and as you exhale, repeat in your mind the word: Relax.

You are in the right place at the right time. Your body and mind are in a highly creative vibration right now. Your mind and your heart are ready to receive whatever it is that you need to know. You have the best possible guidance to allow you to experience the teachings of this Law, and to gather all the important information in any way that it appears.

Whenever you utilize the Law of Increase, you raise your consciousness toward a higher realm. Then, you become a channel that receives the good that awaits you.

Giving praise to God, the Universal Intelligence, is one of the most powerful ways to speed up the delivery of the things you want to manifest, and that's why the Law of Increase and praise are linked. Praise is a powerful activator that opens the door to divine energy. Praise can increase your faith and accelerate your prayers to attract what you desire.

Praise is also considered by many to be the fastest means to acquire your requests. It changes your outlook in life and shifts your vibratory level. When you are focused on the Law of Increase, you are on the lookout for accomplishments that you can applaud in others. This enriches both the giver and the receiver and leaves the receiver with a feeling of having more than they began with.

Praise can bring happiness all around you. Even the cells in your body and the cells of plants respond to praise. Remember energetically we are all one. Practice the vibration of praise and leave everyone around you with the feeling of having and being "more".

Now, to finish your reading, take three deep cleansing breaths, knowing that with each breath you integrate the information you have received. Trust that this is so, and it will be.

Suggested Applications for Today's Law of Flow

Meditate Use the meditation provided for this Law by finding a quiet place to read the selection, or you can listen to the recording of it (if you have purchased the mp3's that go with this book), or use another meditation that appeals to you. (At least 15 minutes)

Gratitude Write at least three things that you are grateful for on this magnificent day. Connect to the feeling of gratitude.

Exercise See yourself having already achieved your goal as you exercise, and praise yourself for it.

Hydrate Drink ½ ounce of pure water per pound of body weight (or 30 ml per kg). 2 glasses upon rising, 2 glasses between breakfast and lunch, 2 glasses between lunch and dinner and 2 after dinner.

Life Insight Leave everyone you meet with an impression of increase. The easiest way to do this all day with everyone you come in contact with is to smile.

Mindful Practice Take a moment, breathe and just be in the present. During your meditation and right now, remember to praise yourself and feel the connection you have with your creator.

Success Strategy Replace negative words (can't, won't, shouldn't, have to) with positive ones (can, will, shall, choose to). Work on having a positive mental attitude and watch how your business improves. Also practice self-audits (evaluations) and see how you can improve different aspects of your business. Remember to praise yourself for all the improvements you make.

Resources *The Law of Increase* from Raymond Holliwell's
　Working With The Law
　How to Win Friends and Influence People by Dale Carnegie

Day 14: The Law Of Self-Knowledge

The Law: You must know yourself. See the value in yourself and this will lead to a greater sense of the flow in all of life.

> *"If you do not conquer self, you will be conquered by self."*
> Napoleon Hill

My Personal Illustration

I have always been very curious about how everything worked and what made people tick. I was especially fascinated about what made ME tick! So I started taking courses, programs, surveys, anything that would give me more information about myself and others. This led me to studying the Enneagram. I learned that I was a Type One with a Two wing and that my instinctual style was one of self-preservation. This gave me some powerful clues for growth and transformation. I gained more insight into my self-defeating patterns and limiting paradigms that were keeping me stuck. I learned that in order to get closer to the essence, the soul, the true nature of me, my type needed to have more fun in life.

Since that revelation, I regularly make a conscious effort to add joyful events and thoughts to my day. Another benefit of learning the Enneagram for myself is that I am able to understand others on a deeper level as well, leading to more harmonious relationships.

Relationship building is vital to business. Now I understand even the most "difficult" person, and how my personality relates to him or her. Insight about personality types has enhanced many business relationships over the years, so I highly recommend its study.

Meditation for The Law Of Self Knowledge

This meditation is a key to unlocking your soul's inner knowing about this Universal Law. It is already in you, so use this time to bring it to your conscious understanding. Read the following meditation slowly.

Take a nice deep breath in through your nose and let it out through your mouth. You are going to let all the tension leave your body, and as you exhale, repeat in your mind the word: Relax.

You are in the right place at the right time. Your body and mind are in a highly creative vibration right now. Your mind and your heart are ready to receive whatever it is that you need to know. You have the best possible guidance to allow you to experience the teachings of this Law, and to gather all the important information in any way that it appears.

This could be called the Law of Self Awareness or Self Consciousness. It could also be called accessing inner truth. You must know yourself and see the value in yourself to grow yourself and this will lead to greater flow in life.

Self-awareness can encourage you to ask questions, to reflect on your behavior, look at the larger picture and invite the answers to come to you. When you are self aware, reality shifts and you can start to take control with the help of your spirit. Becoming self-aware empowers you to make the most wholesome choices in every moment.

What is self? One definition of the self is an individual person as the object of his or her own reflective consciousness. But there are different levels as "self" since we live on three different planes simultaneously. When we think of self, we usually refer to our physical existence because this is what we are most familiar with. But in reality the body is an effect of our thinking patterns, so that is not the best place to explore who we are. Exploring our thoughts and how they affect our body/mind will lead us to much more awareness and knowledge.

Other ways of increasing self-knowledge include looking at ourselves through the eyes of others and observing our own overt behavior and the circumstances in which this behavior occurs. Examining one's own attitudes, beliefs, emotions, desires and other internal mental states can lead to an understanding of one's own nature, abilities, and limitations—all necessary elements to gain insight into oneself.

Ultimately self-knowledge takes us from ordinary and reveals our connection with Source—that eternal well-spring of bliss, that universal impulse which is the very essence of human existence.

Now, to finish your reading, take three deep cleansing breaths, knowing that with each breath you integrate the information you have received. Trust that this is so, and it will be.

Suggested Applications for Today's Law of Flow

Meditate Use the meditation provided for this Law by finding a quiet place to read the selection, or you can listen to the recording of it (if you have purchased the mp3's that go with this book), or use another meditation that appeals to you. (At least 15 minutes)

Gratitude Write at least three things you are grateful for on this magnificent day.

Exercise As you exercise today, notice the vibration you are in. Does it reflect who you are?

Hydrate Drink ½ ounce of pure water per pound of body weight (or 30 ml per kg). 2 glasses upon rising, 2 glasses between breakfast and lunch, 2 glasses between lunch and dinner and 2 after dinner.

Life Insight Get to know yourself. Make a list of your personal strengths and unique talents. What do you love to do with your talents? What is blissful to you? Discover more about who you are via the *Enneagram Institute* Personality Tests or *The Kolbe A™ Index/Instinct* Test. Explore your potential as a human being. Begin to connect with your life's purpose.

Mindful Practice Take a moment, breathe and just be in the present. Watch your vibrations today; notice what you are feeling about what you do and who you are. When you meditate today, pay attention to the "Observer" side of yourself.

Success Strategy Write out the Self Confidence Formula found in Chapter Three on Faith–Visualization of, and Belief in Attainment of Desire–The Second Step Toward Riches from Think and Grow Rich by Napoleon Hill. (To truly integrate this formula into your life, find an accountability partner and write it out for 30 days. If you miss a day, then start all over again until you do 30 days in a row.) Check out an Entrepreneurial Personality Profile or a Leadership Skills Profile. Explore your capabilities in these areas.

Resources *The Masters and the Path* by C.W. Leadbeater
When Things Fall Apart: Heart Advice for Difficult Times
    by Pema Chödrön
The Greatest Salesman In The World by Og Mandino

Day 15: The Law Of Sacrifice

The Law: The Law of Sacrifice says that you cannot get something you want, without giving up something in return. In order to attain something you believe is of greater value, you must give up something you believe is of lesser value.

> *"Don't be afraid to give up the good to go for the great."*
> John D. Rockefeller

My Personal Illustration

This Law takes discipline in order to follow it. Writing this book meant I had to give up some activities, and sometimes it was not easy. Going to plays, attending additional teleseminars and webinars and going to extra Zumba classes was so inviting! Sometimes the activities I gave up were ones of habit and hard to let go of, (especially taking time to organize my email). Just like the book, *Good to Great* by Jim Collins, I had to give up the "good" to get this "great" information into your hands.

Meditation for The Law Of Sacrifice

This meditation is a key to unlocking your soul's inner knowing about this Universal Law. It is already in you, so use this time to bring it to your conscious understanding. Read the following meditation slowly.

Take a nice deep breath in through your nose and let it out through your mouth. You are going to let all the tension leave your body, and as you exhale, repeat in your mind the word: Relax.

You are in the right place at the right time. Your body and mind are in a highly creative vibration right now. Your mind and your heart are ready to receive whatever it is that you need to know. You have the best possible guidance to allow you to experience the teachings of this Law, and to gather all the important information in any way that it appears.

The Law of Sacrifice says that you cannot get something you want, without giving up something in return. Sacrifice does not mean giving up something for nothing; it means giving up one thing for something else you believe is worth more. When you give up something you believe is of lesser value, it opens the way to attain something you believe is of greater value.

This Law is not automatically attractive. It makes you think and may be challenging to apply. Great unhappiness arises when you ignore the Law of Sacrifice and you subconsciously hold the idea in your head that you can have two opposing things at the same time. Take, for example, immediate gratification versus long-term fulfillment. Also if don't really value your goal as much as you think you do, then you will probably not sacrifice anything in order to attain it.

To reach your goals, you must move forward, which means leaving some things behind. When evaluating your dreams, desires, and goals, the question may not be, "What am I willing to do to attain them?" but "What am I willing to give up?" To go after your goals and dreams takes discipline and focus, and you have to make tough decisions about what things you will NOT do. Tune into what you value most and let the Law of Sacrifice turn into a positive element in your life.

Now, to finish your reading, take three deep cleansing breaths, knowing that with each breath you integrate the information you have received. Trust that this is so, and it will be.

Suggested Applications for Today's Law of Flow

Meditate Use the meditation provided for this Law by finding a quiet place to read the selection, or you can listen to the recording of it (if you have purchased the mp3's that go with this book), or use another meditation that appeals to you. (At least 15 minutes)

Gratitude Write at least three things that you are grateful for on this magnificent day. Connect to the feeling of gratitude.

Exercise Ask yourself, how is this exercise benefitting you physically, mentally and spiritually?

Hydrate Drink ½ ounce of pure water per pound of body weight (or 30 ml per kg). 2 glasses upon rising, 2 glasses between breakfast and lunch, 2 glasses between lunch and dinner and 2 after dinner.

Life Insight Give up something in order to get something. Ask yourself, "What habit(s) do I need to change or let go of in order to create something better for myself?" Also ask, "Do I need accountability to stay on track with this change?"

Mindful Practice Take a moment, breathe and just be in the present. Examine your habits today. Ask yourself, "Why did I begin doing this?" and "Does this benefit my body, mind, and spirit?" If you find yourself habitually engaging in activities that do not support your healthy lifestyle, take steps to change those habits.

Success Strategy Self-discipline is in our total control. What one thing are you ready to give up that will free your energy to go towards your current goals? Start tracking your habits over a day and see how you could improve your daily routine.

Resources *The Law of Sacrifice: Lesson 18 from The 21 Irrefutable Laws of Leadership* by John Maxwell

The Law of Sacrifice from Raymond Holliwell's *Working With The Law*

7 Habits of Highly Effective People by Stephen Covey

Day 16: The Law Of Non-Resistance or Detachment

The Law: This Law of Non-Resistance could be called the Law of Detachment. Learn to respond rather than react. Learn how to relax, go with the flow and be in acceptance relinquishing any attachment. Stay focused on the real objective instead of being in resistance.

> *"Resistance is a signal that you are moving into a new area,*
> *however, whatever you resist persists.*
> *Do not resist the resistance."*
> Bob Proctor

My Personal Illustration

When I wrote my first book, I was faced with many obstacles, each one with the potential of stopping me in my tracks. The first one was that I did not type, so I wrote the book by hand and hired a typist. I did not have a book mentor (I didn't even know that there was such a person), so I paid lots of money to various people just to get their opinions. Then, I hired an artist to do all the drawings in color, and when it came time to print the book, the costs of printing a book with color illustrations was impossibly high. So I had to pay the artist to do the entire artwork in black and white instead! With each challenge, one after another, I learned this Law. I accepted each obstacle as it arose without resisting it, but learned from it and saw its gift. I persisted with my goals and self-published a book that became a bestseller.

Here's another example: In my early years, I was quite attached to my beliefs and would get into arguments over them. I obviously did not understand this Law at all back then. (In fact, I did not know the Law even existed.) As I developed more self-knowledge over the years, I saw that there were many truths and I became less attached to my views. Now even when I feel reactive inside, I pause and change my perspective and let it go. Life and my business are so much easier now that I listen to this Law.

Meditation for The Law Of Non-Resistance or Detachment

This meditation is a key to unlocking your soul's inner knowing about this Universal Law. It is already in you, so use this time to bring it to your conscious understanding. Read the following meditation slowly.

Take a nice deep breath in through your nose and let it out through your mouth. You are going to let all the tension leave your body, and as you exhale, repeat in your mind the word: Relax.

You are in the right place at the right time. Your body and mind are in a highly creative vibration right now. Your mind and your heart are ready to receive whatever it is that you need to know. You have the best possible guidance to allow you to experience the teachings of this Law, and to gather all the important information in any way that it appears.

The Law of Non-Resistance or Detachment is probably one of most challenging Laws to master because humans are conditioned to resist and react in all situations instead of responding.

Understanding this Law could be a big turning point and revelation in your life because it calls for you to live with uncertainty and no attachment to the process or the outcome. When you meet with obstacles you must let go of the resistance and allow the difficulties to flow through you without affecting you. See the challenges as stepping stones. Simply flow like a stream or river does. When it encounters a boulder in the way, it doesn't waste its energy on how to move the boulder, it simply flows around it. You too can look for ways to flow around the challenges. The new flow you develop will eventually lead to the vast ocean, tapping into your inner strength and truth. Stay in the flow and get to your end goal in an easier way. Be committed to your goal or vision but unattached to the outcome and flexible in the process. Go with the flow of divine timing.

Realize that reacting and opposing is not strength, it is a weakness. Everything you push against will weaken you and increase the power of the unwanted thing. In many spiritual practices, it is your resistance to what IS that causes your suffering. By changing your perspective, you can usually eliminate the effects of a problem, even if nothing about the problem situation may have changed! Know what you can change and have the wisdom to accept the things you cannot change. The serenity prayer sums this up nicely.

Another way to apply this Law is through meekness. Learning how to be meek is a strength by which you win an argument by refusing to argue. Meekness means you have the strength to move beyond situations that are less than life-giving. This is actually a very powerful position from which to operate. Instead of aligning yourself with disharmony or intolerance, the Law of Non-Resistance connects you with non attached, well-balanced action.

Now, to finish your reading, take three deep cleansing breaths, knowing that with each breath you integrate the information you have received. Trust that this is so, and it will be.

Suggested Applications for Today's Law of Flow

Meditate Use the meditation provided for this Law by finding a quiet place to read the selection, or you can listen to the recording of it (if you have purchased the mp3's that go with this book), or use another meditation that appeals to you. (At least 15 minutes)

Gratitude Write at least three things that you are grateful for on this magnificent day. Connect to the feeling of gratitude.

Exercise As you exercise, be aware of your breath and see if you can stay present while exercising.

Hydrate Drink ½ ounce of pure water per pound of body weight (or 30 ml per kg). 2 glasses upon rising, 2 glasses between breakfast and lunch, 2 glasses between lunch and dinner and 2 after dinner.

Life Insight Keep your awareness in defenselessness. Relinquish the need to defend your point of view. Feel no need to convince or persuade others to accept your point of view. Remain open to all points of view and not be rigidly attached to any of them.

Mindful Practice Take a moment, breathe and just be in the present. Today commit to staying grounded in the present. Whenever you find yourself worrying about the past or feeling fearful about the future, take three deep breaths to bring yourself back to the here and now.

Success Strategy Turn every challenge into an opportunity. These are the best opportunities for you to learn and grow. It's all about how you decide to approach them. List how obstacles from your past have actually led to more positive things: new knowledge, inspiration, unexpected opportunities, etc.

Resources *The Game of Life and How to Play It* by Florence Scovel Shinn *Esoteric Healing A Treatise On The Seven Rays Volume IV* by Alice A. Bailey The Law of *Non-Resistance* from Raymond Holliwell's *Working With The Law*

Day 17: The Law Of Obedience

The Law: The Law of Obedience simply states that you can only achieve success if you obey the Universal Laws and the laws of nature.

> *"We must all obey the great law of change. It is the most powerful law of nature."*
> Edmund Burke

My Personal Illustration

Like most of us, I bumped up against many of the Laws as I was "learning the ropes" of this earth school. The Laws protect us in the sense that they keep the vast field of existence orderly, which is heaven's first Law (see *Your Invisible Power* by Genevieve Behrand).

As a child I learned that taking gum from a store was a no-no because I did not give anything of value (money) in exchange for it. So I learned that I had to be obedient to the Law of Compensation. I also learned about the laws of nature when I touched a hot element on the stove. Now that I think of it, much of my learning was not through obedience to these Laws at first, but by violating them!

I know that this applied to my business as well. In the beginning I was not aware of the Laws. So I went through many lean times with my lack of knowledge and lack of connection with Source. Not being compliant with this Law, I had to rely on my persistence in order to keep going many times.

Meditation for The Law Of Obedience

This meditation is a key to unlocking your soul's inner knowing about this Universal Law. It is already in you, so use this time to bring it to your conscious understanding. Read the following meditation slowly.

Take a nice deep breath in through your nose and let it out through your mouth. You are going to let all the tension leave your body, and as you exhale, repeat in your mind the word: Relax.

You are in the right place at the right time. Your body and mind are in a highly creative vibration right now. Your mind and your heart are ready to receive whatever it is that you need to know. You have the best possible guidance to allow you to experience the teachings of this Law, and to gather all the important information in any way that it appears.

The Law of Obedience simply states that you can only achieve success if you know how to use the Universal Laws and the laws of nature. When a farmer plants seeds and is obedient to these Universal Laws, then nature reaps an abundant harvest.

Laws are always operating in your life, and a "mistake" is falling short of or disobeying a Law or going against your better knowledge. According to Raymond Holliwell, when one misuses, misunderstands, inverts or violates a Law, this mistake is known as a sin. It could also be considered a disconnection from your true self, your higher self, the "I am" aspect.

However, when you learn about how these Laws operate and align your thoughts and actions with them, you can use them to your advantage. You can then consciously create your reality and improve every aspect of your life.

It may take discipline and persistence and may not be easy to do, but it is truly rewarding. Align yourself with the way the Laws operate, and see what a difference it makes to be in harmony with the universal forces at work in creation.

Now, to finish your reading, take three deep cleansing breaths, knowing that with each breath you integrate the information you have received. Trust that this is so, and it will be.

Suggested Applications for Today's Law of Flow

Meditate Use the meditation provided for this Law by finding a quiet place to read the selection, or you can listen to the recording of it (if you have purchased the mp3's that go with this book), or use another meditation that appeals to you. (At least 15 minutes)

Gratitude Write at least three things that you are grateful for on this magnificent day. Connect to the feeling of gratitude.

Exercise As you exercise, send messages of kindness and love to any area of your body that feels any discomfort.

Hydrate Drink ½ ounce of pure water per pound of body weight (or 30 ml per kg). 2 glasses upon rising, 2 glasses between breakfast and lunch, 2 glasses between lunch and dinner and 2 after dinner.

Life Insight Reflect on how you are using excuses. Are you mistaking excuses for credible reasons for not doing something? This one requires self honesty and might be a challenge. Sometimes it is harder to be honest with ourselves than actually doing what we are trying to avoid.

Mindful Practice Take a moment, breathe and just be in the present. When you settle in for meditation or in a quiet moment, pay attention to any areas in your life where you may feel any disconnection from your true self. Feel free to journal about any thoughts that appear.

Success Strategy To enhance your business greatly, read the seven-page article on "Decision" by Bob Proctor. Google it and you will find a PDF online.

Resources *The Law of Obedience* from Raymond Holliwell's book *Working With The Law*

A Path with Heart: A Guide Through the Perils and Promises of Spiritual Life by Jack Kornfield

Day 18: The Law Of Forgiveness

The Law: Forgiveness permits you to be in harmony with yourself and allows you to wish everyone well.

> *"Always forgive your enemies;*
> *nothing annoys them so much."*
> Oscar Wilde

My Personal Illustration

In business it is very easy to get involved with "get-rich-quick ideas". Well, I was always curious about what people had to offer and more than once went into "investments" where I lost everything. When it happened, I felt very resentful and was not very happy with these people. I certainly had no intention of ever forgiving them for wiping out my savings. Then I learned what money really was (just an idea) and through further understanding of some spiritual teachings and this Law, I forgave those people. I also had to forgive myself and gather all the learning through the experience of loss. To be successful in business, working with this Law is truly freeing.

Meditation for The Law Of Forgiveness

This meditation is a key to unlocking your soul's inner knowing about this Universal Law. It is already in you, so use this time to bring it to your conscious understanding. Read the following meditation slowly.

Take a nice deep breath in through your nose and let it out through your mouth. You are going to let all the tension leave your body, and as you exhale, repeat in your mind the word: Relax.

You are in the right place at the right time. Your body and mind are in a highly creative vibration right now. Your mind and your heart are ready to receive whatever it is that you need to know. You have the best possible guidance to allow you to experience the teachings of this Law, and to gather all the important information in any way that it appears.

Forgiveness of another (or yourself) restores the truth of one's own being. It permits you to be in harmony with yourself and allows you to wish everyone well. It brings freedom, transparency, and the renewal of life energies.

All experiences have their purpose in the progression of your life. Understand though, that you invite people and situations into your life so that you may create, experience, learn, heal, and/or grow. So not all of these people and situations may automatically be positive at first. Ultimately though, they all have the potential to be positive experiences, and the Law of Forgiveness is a powerful tool to do so.

A big caveat here: Forgiveness is not about condoning any encounters that may hurt you, but it is an understanding of why it occurred and the process of completely letting it go through that awareness. Continuing to hold thoughts of guilt and resentment in your mind leads to inertia and resistance, as these lower vibrations impact your body. You are the one being affected and this blocks or impedes any spiritual connection and prevents you from getting what you desire in life. When you forgive, it breaks that bond, removes the block and frees up your creative energy that reconnects you to Source.

Forgiveness for self is vital, and truly, that's what forgiveness is all about. When you can look at yourself in the mirror and say, "I love you," you are on your way to experiencing the life you desire.

Now, to finish your reading, take three deep cleansing breaths, knowing that with each breath you integrate the information you have received. Trust that this is so, and it will be.

Suggested Applications for Today's Law of Flow

Meditate Use the meditation provided for this Law by finding a quiet place to read the selection, or you can listen to the recording of it (if you have purchased the mp3's that go with this book), or use another meditation that appeals to you. (At least 15 minutes)

Gratitude Write at least three things that you are grateful for on this magnificent day. Connect to the feeling of gratitude.

Exercise As you exercise, repeat the affirmation, "I love and accept myself unconditionally."

Hydrate Drink ½ ounce of pure water per pound of body weight (or 30 ml per kg). 2 glasses upon rising, 2 glasses between breakfast and lunch, 2 glasses between lunch and dinner and 2 after dinner.

Life Insight Practice forgiveness. If you need to forgive anyone, repeat these words, "I forgive you completely. The interaction that occurred between us is now complete. I honor the spirit within you." Feel free to use whatever words work for you.

Mindful Practice Take a moment, breathe and just be in the present. Let go of any thoughts of guilt and resentment in your mind, as it blocks or slows any spiritual connection and prevents you from getting what you desire in life. Forgive yourself for one significant thing today, and let go of the negative thoughts associated with them.

Success Strategy What are anger and resentment doing to you? Where do you find those two things in your business or in your personal life? Take those issues and practice the forgiveness exercise from the Life Insight section. Your energy will soar.

Resources *The Law of Forgiveness: Tap in to the Positive Power of Forgiveness—and Attract Good Things to Your Life* by Connie Domino
Radical Forgiveness by Colin C. Tipping
The Law of Forgiveness from Raymond Holliwell's *Working With The Law*

Day 19: The Law Of Reciprocity

The Law: This Law flows from the energy of the Golden Rule: Do unto others as you would have others do unto you.

> *"Always recognize that human individuals are ends, and do not use them as means to your end."*
> Immanuel Kant

My Personal Illustration

I use this Law in a few ways. I sponsor four foster children around the world without any expectation that they will repay me. I just like to know that they have a chance to go to school and have a better life thanks to my contributions. It uplifts me to help another human being. I support multiple charities with the hopes that the people on the receiving end can make some improvements in their lives.

Another way I use this Law is when I offer my services to others with no expectation that they are going to compensate me, they receive a benefit from that interaction. When I have friends or family who are experiencing difficulties, I help in whatever way I can–again with no expectation that they have to do anything in return. The same goes for my clients. I give them more than they have paid me for, and many times I will give away my books or health charts, just for the joy of giving.

I know that the universe keeps track and when lovely things happen to me unexpectedly, I am sure it must be from all the times I have given over the years.

Meditation for The Law Of Reciprocity

This meditation is a key to unlocking your soul's inner knowing about this Universal Law. It is already in you, so use this time to bring it to your conscious understanding. Read the following meditation slowly.

Take a nice deep breath in through your nose and let it out through your mouth. You are going to let all the tension leave your body, and as you exhale, repeat in your mind the word: Relax.

You are in the right place at the right time. Your body and mind are in a highly creative vibration right now. Your mind and your heart are ready to receive whatever it is that you need to know. You have the best possible guidance to allow you to experience the teachings of this Law, and to gather all the important information in any way that it appears.

The Law of Reciprocity refers to responding to a positive action with another positive action, rewarding caring deeds with more caring deeds. It means that people are frequently much nicer and much more cooperative in response to friendly actions. This Law flows from the energy of the Golden Rule: Do Unto Others As You Would Have Others Do Unto You.

The Law of Reciprocity states that all transmissions of energy result in a return of energy in kind, but rarely right away and sometimes from another source. And so those who help you may not be those same ones you help! Acts of contribution, big and small, create a bank of reciprocity. Paradoxically, it is when you help or serve others without expectation of reward or pay, that you invoke the power of this Law. Also what you broadcast into the universe, whether it is negative or positive, is a credit due to come back to you. Your credits may be returned promptly, or they may collect and be returned at a later time.

Another way to utilize this Law is by doing more than what you are paid for. Once again, this helps you bank deposits with the universe and eventually this insures you a return far out of proportion to the service you rendered. Imagine the feeling of giving without expectation of return! Feel how it makes a change in your body. Notice where that feeling is for you.

Now, to finish your reading, take three deep cleansing breaths, knowing that with each breath you integrate the information you have received. Trust that this is so, and it will be.

Suggested Applications for Today's Law of Flow

Meditate Use the meditation provided for this Law by finding a quiet place to read the selection, or you can listen to the recording of it (if you have purchased the mp3's that go with this book), or use another meditation that appeals to you. (At least 15 minutes)

Gratitude Write at least three things that you are grateful for on this magnificent day. Connect to the feeling of gratitude.

Exercise As you exercise, send love to everyone you know and imagine them in perfect health.

Hydrate Drink ½ ounce of pure water per pound of body weight (or 30 ml per kg). 2 glasses upon rising, 2 glasses between breakfast and lunch, 2 glasses between lunch and dinner and 2 after dinner.

Life Insight Bring a gift to whomever you encounter today. The gift may be a compliment, a flower, or a prayer. Today, when you give something to everyone you come into contact with, you will begin the process of circulating joy, wealth and affluence in your life and in the lives of others.

Mindful Practice Take a moment, breathe and just be in the present. Think win/win in all the situations you come across today. Treat everyone you see today as "the most important person".

Success Strategy Write or read aloud *Chapter 14 The Impression of Increase from The Science of Getting Rich* by Wallace D. Wattles. (If you feel you really want to integrate this chapter, then find an accountability partner and write it out or read it aloud with your partner for 30 days. If you miss a day, then start all over again until you do thirty days in a row.) Speak highly of everyone in their presence and when referring to them to others.

Resources Walking Between the Worlds: The Science of Compassion
     by Gregg Braden
     Influence–the Psychology of Persuasion by Robert B. Cialdini

Day 20: The Law Of Creativity

The Law: Creativity is the force that resides within you; the Creator's energy expresses itself more fully through your uniqueness. All possibility is seeking expression. You are a co-creator.

> *"The inner fire is the most important thing*
> *mankind possesses."*
> Edith Södergran

My Personal Illustration

My creativity has manifested different things over the years. When I was younger, I used my creativity to produce all sorts of crafts, everything from pottery to jewelry. My creativity dried up at times and then it would blossom again in a completely different medium. Books, programs and audios now seem to be the new channel for my creativity. Utilizing the creative faculties of my conscious mind has helped tremendously. I have to admit that when I am in a totally creative space, all time disappears and I am lost in the bliss of no-thing (nothing).

In business or in whatever creative endeavor, just remember to have fun with it. It is your birthright to create!

Your Reading Meditation for The Law Of Creativity

This meditation is a key to unlocking your soul's inner knowing about this Universal Law. It is already in you, so use this time to bring it to your conscious understanding. Read the following meditation slowly.

Take a nice deep breath in through your nose and let it out through your mouth. You are going to let all the tension leave your body, and as you exhale, repeat in your mind the word: Relax.

You are in the right place at the right time. Your body and mind are in a highly creative vibration right now. Your mind and your heart are ready to receive whatever it is that you need to know. You have the best possible guidance to allow you to experience the teachings of this Law, and to gather all the important information in any way that it appears.

You are a creator, you are a creative being. Creativity is the force which resides within you and The Creator's energy expresses itself more fully through your uniqueness. All possibility is seeking expression, and life is about expression.

We create no matter what, but we either create by design or default. If we are not managing our minds, then we are creating our life by default 96% of the time. If we are not cultivating new habits (paradigms), the old ones run automatically (even without our awareness). We need to learn to focus on creating new desires of what we really want and to utilize our creativity in a positive direction. Remember, if we are not consciously creating, then our subconscious patterns are creating for us.

You have been endowed with six creative faculties to help you manifest energy from the invisible to an earthly, or physical state of matter. You have been gifted with a reasoning facility, perception, will, memory, intuition and imagination in your conscious mind. These give you access to the mind of God, a higher order. You can use these faculties to co-create what you really desire.

This Law simply states that by bringing creations into the world, you are allowing yourself and others to benefit from an increase in energy, a raised consciousness. Ever notice that in a state of creation, you are so present with what you are doing that you forget about yourself? You forget about you, you become nobody, you become nothing, you become no time, you become pure consciousness in that moment. Inspiration comes when you are connected to spirit. True success is measured by how efficiently and effortlessly you have learned to co-create with the universe and live a life in successful creative expression.

Now, to finish your reading, take three deep cleansing breaths, knowing that with each breath you integrate the information you have received. Trust that this is so, and it will be.

Suggested Applications for Today's Law of Flow

Meditate Use the meditation provided for this Law by finding a quiet place to read the selection, or you can listen to the recording of it (if you have purchased the mp3's that go with this book), or use another meditation that appeals to you. (At least 15 minutes)

Gratitude Write at least three things that you are grateful for on this magnificent day. Connect to the feeling of gratitude.

Exercise As you exercise be creative today, either change your exercise routine or do something wild and crazy.

Hydrate Drink ½ ounce of pure water per pound of body weight (or 30 ml per kg). 2 glasses upon rising, 2 glasses between breakfast and lunch, 2 glasses between lunch and dinner and 2 after dinner.

Life Insight Consider an activity that really excites you. Make the commitment to engage in that activity for some time every day. Witness how time stands still when you indulge your passion and you become deeply rooted in the present.

Mindful Practice Take a moment, breathe and just be in the present. Investigate and develop the intellectual or creative faculties of your mind. If you wish, meditate on a candle flame to develop your concentration and focus (in other words, your creative faculty of will). Pay attention to that aspect of you that is the "Observer."

Success Strategy Imagine your ideal life where your goal has been reached and things are how you want them. What is life like? Describe it in detail. Use all your senses in this description. Then imagine five alternative methods of achieving your goal. Let your imagination go wild. Create an ideas book for your big ideas, thoughts and goals.

Resources *The Courage to Create* by Rollo May
Flow: The Psychology of Optimal Experience by Mihaly Csikszentmihalyi
Creativity: Flow and the Psychology of Discovery and Invention by Mihaly Csikszentmihalyi
Six Thinking Hats by Edward De Bono
The Artist's Way: A Spiritual Path to Higher Creativity by Julia Cameron
The Mind Map Book: How to Use Radiant Thinking to Maximize Your Brain's Untapped Potential by Tony Buzan and Barry Buzan

Day 21: The Law Of Reflection

The Law: This Law has two interpretations. One is that we stop, pause or reflect and let the events we have encountered catch up with us and get integrated. The other interpretation is that when we look at other people around us, they can be reflecting back to us things we are not quite ready to see inside ourselves.

> *"By three methods we may learn wisdom: First, by reflec-*
> *tion, which is noblest; Second, by imitation, which is easiest;*
> *and third by experience, which is the bitterest."*
> Confucius

My Personal Illustration

I first began meditating in my twenties and it has been a part of my spiritual practice ever since. One experience I had while meditating was being filled with total unconditional love on a vibrational level that was so fine that my dense body vibration had a hard time letting it in. I began to cry with the disparity in vibration. But I knew and experienced that love so greatly that I knew that no matter what transgression I was involved with, I would be forgiven through that unconditional love. I also knew this to be true of all mankind. This understanding was not to invite any transgressions but to know that despite the mistakes, total unconditional love remained. This is just one of the many gifts of the practice of quiet reflection.

Using this Law as a mirror is quite a practical tool, since I am still working on a few habits I am not happy with. I see them ever so clearly in the people around me. Every time I am irritated, I make it a practice to look within and see what part of me is still in need of growth or healing.

Years ago, when I started back to school as an older adult, I was with many young folks in the same class. One young man started to irritate the heck out of me, and I couldn't figure out why. It got so bad that I could not be around him, which, in a small class, is difficult. Knowing I had to be near him all year, I realized I had to go inside and find out what was bothering me so much.

After much self-inquiry and meditation, I realized that I was really scared going back to school after being away from a structured school setting for over 15 years. As soon as I understood what I was feeling, I saw that he also was frightened and his "irritating" actions was mirroring this feeling back to me that I had not been ready to acknowledge. My irritation with him vanished with this realization.

When it comes to business, the bottom line with this Law is that it is imperative to go within if you really want to be a successful entrepreneur.

Meditation for The Law Of Reflection

This meditation is a key to unlocking your soul's inner knowing about this Universal Law. It is already in you, so use this time to bring it to your conscious understanding. Read the following meditation slowly.

Take a nice deep breath in through your nose and let it out through your mouth. You are going to let all the tension leave your body, and as you exhale, repeat in your mind the word: Relax.

You are in the right place at the right time. Your body and mind are in a highly creative vibration right now. Your mind and your heart are ready to receive whatever it is that you need to know. You have the best possible guidance to allow you to experience the teachings of this Law, and to gather all the important information in any way that it appears.

The Law of Reflection says that no matter what we do in life, there is always the need to stop or take a breather and integrate the events we have encountered. Reflection is one way we can do this. Life comes at us fast and for many of us, we have to respond to shifts in direction all day long. Look at your workload and determine when and where you can spend time in meditation and contemplation.

People everywhere seek peace, happiness and freedom from life's entanglements, without realizing that what they seek is already within themselves. The word meditation in Tibetan literally means "to become familiar with." So when you sit in meditation, with your eyes closed, you have eliminated the environment, you are no longer focused on time and you begin to observe the steady stream of thoughts. You are meditating to become familiar with your real self.

There are many ways to get into this state. Becoming mindful and concentrating on your breath can bring you into a more reflective state. Another great way to generate this Law is by being in nature. Nature itself teaches you to slow down. You can also invoke this Law by journaling your findings and being perceptive and sensitive to any shifts in your consciousness.

The Law of Reflection is also an inward journey where we can discover that we are essentially spiritual beings rooted in God or the One Mind. When we are still, we do not have to apologize, justify ourselves, or impress people. We can let go of the ego aspect of self. Rather, in stillness we reconnect with our being, our real nature, our true Self. This connection is essential for living a life of flow.

There is another way to look at this Law of Reflection. When we think of a mirror we can see our reflection in the mirror. When we look at other people around us, they can be reflecting back to us things we are not quite ready to see inside ourselves. What reflections of other people and other things are affecting you? When someone or something annoys you, identify what is really upsetting you about them or it. Now look deep inside yourself and identify that irritation inside of you. Conversely, when you are with someone who makes you joyful or you really appreciate an object, look deep inside yourself to see what it mirrors to you that you like about yourself. Enhance these qualities and you will attract more people with these characteristics to come into your life.

It is so important to realize that the reflection you have identified, you cannot change in the other person or object. Instead, ask yourself what is this person or situation teaching me and determine what is the message. What is the reflection that is being mirrored back and why? If it irritates you or you don't like what's happening outside, only you can make the change, inside of YOU. Just look within and change yourself and watch the reflection change. When you do this, these situations and people will disappear from your life and life will flow for you.

See reflections as continual growth opportunities: fascinating, exciting *openings to become who you really are as you strive to remember you as part of the Oneness. By understanding the Law of Reflection, you can expand your spiritual growth by looking at what life is telling you through others.*

Now, to finish your reading, take three deep cleansing breaths, knowing that with each breath you integrate the information you have received. Trust that this is so, and it will be.

Suggested Applications for Today's Law of Flow

Meditate Use the meditation provided for this Law by finding a quiet place to read the selection, or you can listen to the recording of it (if you have purchased the mp3's that go with this book), or use another meditation that appeals to you. (At least 15 minutes)

Gratitude Write at least three things that you are grateful for on this magnificent day. Connect to the feeling of gratitude.

Exercise Go outside for your exercise today. Walking consciously, slowly, and deliberately will aid in discovering the rhythms of nature. Notice the sights, sounds, smells and stillness that would normally be lost to you by hurrying.

Hydrate Drink ½ ounce of pure water per pound of body weight (or 30 ml per kg). 2 glasses upon rising, 2 glasses between breakfast and lunch, 2 glasses between lunch and dinner and 2 after dinner.

Life Insight Take time throughout your day to become more mindful and concentrate on your breath as many times as you can. Or, if you wish to focus on the mirroring aspect of this Law, your focus is to become aware of your interactions with others. What aspects of YOU are being reflected there?

Mindful Practice Take a moment, breathe and just be in the present. For the mindful reflection, take an extra five to ten minutes out of your day and go into a quiet state of reflection. This can be added to your regular meditation if you wish or simply reflect during the day as needed. If you feel you need more time, just get up ten minutes earlier and you will have created the extra time to take the ten minutes in reflection.

For the mirroring reflection, take a look at what is either irritating you or pleasing you in the people around you. Ask yourself "What is this person teaching me?" Look at the person and consider the lesson to be learned. What is the reflection that is being mirrored back to you and why? Then (here's the magical part) make the change inside and watch the reflection change outside.

Success Strategy Write out by hand *Chapter Eight: Serenity* in *As a Man Thinketh* by James Allen. (If you feel you really want to integrate this chapter then find an accountability partner and write it out for 30 days. If you miss a day, then start all over again until you do thirty days in a row. If you are needing the calming effect of this chapter in your life, then write it out for 90 days.)

Resources *A New Earth: Awakening to Your Life's Purpose*
　　　by Eckhart Tolle
The Power of Now: A Guide to Spiritual Enlightenment
　　　by Eckhart Tolle
Tao Te Ching by Lao Tzu

Day 22: The Law Of Intention or Deliberate Creation

The Law: This Law of Intention could be called the Law of Deliberate Creation. Intention is the process of getting clear and specific on what you want and planning it out. Intent alone is very powerful, because intent is desire without attachment to the outcome.

> *"We are what we think. All that we are arises with our thoughts. With our thoughts, we make the world."*
> Buddha

My Personal Illustration

This Law has totally worked in my business but this illustration will be from my personal life as it demonstrates one of my most passionate intentions.

There used to be quite a stigma around having a child out of wedlock. Unfortunately I became pregnant when it was still unacceptable. So I was forced to give up my daughter for adoption, since I was young and had no financial or family support. As time passed and I got back on my feet, I resolved that I would find her. I took all sorts of actions over the years all with no results, but I kept my faith. Every year I would put an ad in the paper on her birthday; I registered with all the underground agencies that were working on matches. Finally when the government adoption agency let me register my name saying I wanted contact, I did so with the intention that she would also register and that we would be re-united.

I had every intention of having her back in my life and I kept the faith. I would visualize little scenarios in my mind with her being present. I would see myself introducing her to all my friends. My belief level was that it had already happened–that's how strong my intention was.

One year, the day after Mother's Day, I received the long-dreamed-of call from Children's Aid. I was ecstatic that my intention to re-unite was finally going to materialize. We quickly bypassed all the red tape and within a few weeks were able to embrace after 24 years!

What I didn't expect was not only did I re-unite with her, I also saw my two granddaughters for the first time at the ages of four and six. My intention all along was to bring the family back together again and we were able to continue growing together from that point on. (Now many years later, one of my granddaughters has a child, so now I am a great-grandmother to a lovely little boy.) The Law of Intention works!

Meditation for The Law Of Intention or Deliberate Creation

This meditation is a key to unlocking your soul's inner knowing about this Universal Law. It is already in you, so use this time to bring it to your conscious understanding. Read the following meditation slowly.

Take a nice deep breath in through your nose and let it out through your mouth. You are going to let all the tension leave your body, and as you exhale, repeat in your mind the word: Relax.

You are in the right place at the right time. Your body and mind are in a highly creative vibration right now. Your mind and your heart are ready to receive whatever it is that you need to know. You have the best possible guidance to allow you to experience the teachings of this Law, and to gather all the important information in any way that it appears.

Intention is a conscious thought process. It means getting clear on what you want internally and consciously planning it out, deliberately creating it. Be really specific. It is not about hoping, it is about a deeply felt knowing. Intent is the real power behind desire because desire for most people is attention with attachment. Intent, on the other hand, is very potent, because intent is desire without any attachment to the outcome. Intention lays the groundwork for the effortless, spontaneous flow of pure potentiality that seeks expression from the unmanifest to the manifest.

Intention triggers the transformation of energy and information into what you put your attention on. It organizes an infinite number of events to materialize your desires. You may have fallen in love with your desire, but it is really intent that moves it toward you. Never struggle against the present with intention. Accept the present and focus on the actions you can take today that will manifest your intentions for the future.

If you are not being intentional, then you are creating your life by default 96% of the time. Remember, if you are not deliberately creating, then your subconscious patterns are creating for you.

An intention with faith is like an arrow shot from a bow. Nothing can deflect it. So be on purpose when you co-create.

Now, to finish your reading, take three deep cleansing breaths, knowing that with each breath you integrate the information you have received. Trust that this is so, and it will be.

Suggested Applications for Today's Law of Flow

Meditate Use the meditation provided for this Law by finding a quiet place to read the selection, or you can listen to the recording of it (if you have purchased the mp3's that go with this book), or use another meditation that appeals to you. (At least 15 minutes)

Gratitude Write at least three things that you are grateful for on this magnificent day. Connect to the feeling of gratitude.

Exercise What do you intend to feel as a result of your exercise today? Think clearly about that, and see what you create because of your intention.

Hydrate Drink ½ ounce of pure water per pound of body weight (or 30 ml per kg). 2 glasses upon rising, 2 glasses between breakfast and lunch, 2 glasses between lunch and dinner and 2 after dinner.

Life Insight Set three intentions: one intention for your journey toward perfect health, one intention in your business, and one intention for one of your relationships.

Mindful Practice Take a moment, breathe and just be in the present. Notice the expression of the infinite organizing power in every blade of grass, in every blossom, in every cell of your body, in everything. Take some time out and notice the results of intentions in your environment and in your daily life. What intentions are you consciously and deliberately setting, and what intentions are you setting out of habit?

Success Strategy Get crystal clear about what you intend. Write out a goal card and take it with you and look at it often throughout the day assuming the feeling that you already possess it.

Resources *The Power of Intention: Learning to Co-create Your World Your Way* by Dr. Wayne W. Dyer

The Intention Experiment: Using Your Thoughts to Change Your Life and the World by Lynne McTaggart

Day 23: The Law Of Visualization

The Law: Visualizing–feeding your mind with clear, exciting, emotional pictures–is a key component to manifesting your desires, since the subconscious mind thinks in pictures.

"A picture is worth a thousand words."
Napoleon Bonaparte

My Personal Illustration

In one of my businesses that involves the sale of wellness products, there is a point system that sets the income level each month. The highest amount of points is 10,000 and I would visualize that total or higher each month. I knew if I reached that goal each month, my income would cover all my basic expenses. So I visualized that amount each month. I had to keep my faith, though, since there would be some months that the points would be half the amount I was visualizing and there were only a few days before the end of the month! When I kept the vision, the points would climb over 10,000 every time. But on the months that I stopped visualizing and let my five senses take over and believe what I saw on the computer screen to be the reality, I would not make those necessary points. I would buy into what my senses saw and not keep up with my visualizations, faith and gratitude that those points were already in place. I noticed my heart was not into it as well during those months.

Here's an important point I learned: when I visualized anything, I had to involve my heart, my will, and change my energetic vibration to invoke the Law of Attraction (Day 12). It was vital to keep the vision even though the physical reality appeared as if it did not support it. When I did that, I was able to manifest what I saw from the inside out. Every time I did this, it worked. This is so important for any business.

Meditation for The Law Of Visualization

This meditation is a key to unlocking your soul's inner knowing about this Universal Law. It is already in you, so use this time to bring it to your conscious understanding. Read the following meditation slowly.

Take a nice deep breath in through your nose and let it out through your mouth. You are going to let all the tension leave your body, and as you exhale, repeat in your mind the word: Relax.

You are in the right place at the right time. Your body and mind are in a highly creative vibration right now. Your mind and your heart are ready to receive whatever it is that you need to know. You have the best possible guidance to allow you to experience the teachings of this Law, and to gather all the important information in any way that it appears.

Visualizing is the great secret of success. Since the subconscious mind thinks in pictures, visualizing is a key component to manifesting your desires. You possess more power and greater possibilities than you realize, and visualizing is one of the greatest of these powers.

A key tool in visualization is your imagination. Your imagination is your preview of all of life's possibilities. Get your idea crystal clear in your mind and make it into a vivid image. Believe and feel that it is possible and use the power of repetition to make it come into reality. The more frequently you repeat a clear mental picture with an emotional (heart) connection of what you desire, the more rapidly it will appear as part of your reality. When the picture in your head matches the picture in your heart then the Law of Attraction is invoked.

Early morning and before going to sleep are good times to visualize since you are more in an alpha brain wave state then, and your subconscious mind receives your affirmations or images best. Making time for meditation throughout the day is another good way to feed your subconscious mind.

The Law of Visualization brings you whatever you vividly and intensely imagine, but like all the Laws, it is impersonal and allows you the freedom of choice. So you get to choose whether to apply this Law to something you desire or something you don't want.

Affirmations go hand in hand with visualization as we can add sound to the images. Repeat them in the present tense with belief, feeling and emotion. If you don't repeat them with emotion, like joy, pride, or excitement, they will not produce results. You can also choose to record your affirmations in an audio device and use them while you sleep. Your conscious mind is disconnected from your subconscious mind during sleep and thus your affirmations go directly into your subconscious mind.

In Genevieve Behrend's words, "Your object in visualizing is to bring things into regular order both mentally and physically…In other words, when your understanding grasps the power to visualize your heart's desire and hold it with your will, it attracts to you all things requisite to the fulfillment of that picture by the harmonious vibrations of the Law of Attraction. You realize that since Order is Heaven's first Law, and visualization places things in their natural element, then it must be a heavenly thing to visualize."

You are creating from the formless substance by means of your individual thought power and manifesting it on the physical plane. Feel the pure potentiality of your thought vibration as it aligns with the power that manifests everything in the universe.

Now, to finish your reading, take three deep cleansing breaths, knowing that with each breath you integrate the information you have received. Trust that this is so, and it will be.

Suggested Applications for Today's Law of Flow

Meditate Use the meditation provided for this Law by finding a quiet place to read the selection, or you can listen to the recording of it (if you have purchased the mp3's that go with this book), or use another meditation that appeals to you. (At least 15 minutes)

Gratitude Write at least three things that you are grateful for on this magnificent day. Connect to the feeling of gratitude.

Exercise As you exercise visualize your ideal body.

Hydrate Drink ½ ounce of pure water per pound of body weight (or 30 ml per kg). 2 glasses upon rising, 2 glasses between breakfast and lunch, 2 glasses between lunch and dinner and 2 after dinner.

Life Insight Visualize your dreams and desires. Utilize all your senses as you visualize. See, hear, taste, smell and feel every aspect of your dream. Know that everything is created twice, once in your mind and then again physically.

Mindful Practice Take a moment, breathe and just be in the present. Make a commitment to use your imagination to visualize something that you desire.

Success Strategy List three things you want to manifest and visualize them as if they are already completed using all your sensory factors and assuming the feeling that you already have them.

Resources Your Invisible Power, Chapter 1- Order Of Visualization by Genevieve Behrend

Basic Laws of Cosmic Power by Eric Butterworth

Day 24: The Law Of Action

The Law: Action that supports your desires allows you to manifest things on earth and get the results you want. Action is definitely the key to success.

> *"In order to carry a positive action we must*
> *develop here a positive vision."*
> Dalai Lama

My Personal Illustration

The Law of Action is necessary in order to manifest on the physical plane. I could have kept visualizing any of the health and wellness books I have written, but without action they would not have been written. I needed to be in action, especially near the end as I had to coordinate editors, layout artists, typesetters and printers. I had to maintain my attitude of "I can" and stick with my passion to educate and simplify a very complicated subject. With daily actions, the books materialized and I achieved my bigger goal: helping hundreds of people with their health challenges.

Once again I am in action for this book. In the age of the internet, the process is quite different, but action is required in order to make it a reality. For any part of our business action is important. I love the saying by Pablo Picasso, "Action is the foundational key to success".

Meditation for The Law Of Action

This meditation is a key to unlocking your soul's inner knowing about this Universal Law. It is already in you, so use this time to bring it to your conscious understanding. Read the following meditation slowly.

Take a nice deep breath in through your nose and let it out through your mouth. You are going to let all the tension leave your body, and as you exhale, repeat in your mind the word: Relax.

You are in the right place at the right time. Your body and mind are in a highly creative vibration right now. Your mind and your heart are ready to receive whatever it is that you need to know. You have the best possible guidance to allow you to experience the teachings of this Law, and to gather all the important information in any way that it appears.

The Law of Action states that you must move in the direction of your dreams in order to achieve them. You must engage in some action that supports what you think about and/or dream about. It is your burning desire that drives your action. Your passion will move you into inspired action. You must engage in actions that support your thoughts, dreams, emotions and words.

Action allows you to manifest things on earth and make them yours. Knowledge with positive action can create a powerful force. The Law of Action says that action is always necessary to achieve the results you desire in life. To manifest the dreams you desire, you must engage in actions which support your desires and dreams, as well as your thoughts, emotions, and words. You need to gain mastery over your thoughts and program your mind with "I can."

When you immediately follow your decisions with action, doors begin to open. Self-motivation mobilizes you from the inside out. Once you have made a decision, act with enthusiasm, courage, persistence, passion and purpose. See your actions co-creating all that you desire as you align with the power that manifests everything in the universe.

Now, to finish your reading, take three deep cleansing breaths, knowing that with each breath you integrate the information you have received. Trust that this is so, and it will be.

Suggested Applications for Today's Law of Flow

Meditate Use the meditation provided for this Law by finding a quiet place to read the selection, or you can listen to the recording of it (if you have purchased the mp3's that go with this book), or use another meditation that appeals to you. (At least 15 minutes)

Gratitude Write at least three things that you are grateful for on this magnificent day. Connect to the feeling of gratitude.

Exercise As you exercise today, commit to making exercise a personal habit, even when your 30 days of this plan is complete.

Hydrate Drink ½ ounce of pure water per pound of body weight (or 30 ml per kg). 2 glasses upon rising, 2 glasses between breakfast and lunch, 2 glasses between lunch and dinner and 2 after dinner.

Life Insight Do or find what you love. It is easy to be in action when you have a passion for something. Explore the Passion Test if you are unclear about your values and loves. You can find the test in the book *The Passion Test: The Effortless Path to Discovering Your Destiny* by Janet Bray Attwood and Chris Attwood. Or find a coach who will take through the process to find your loves and passions.

Mindful Practice Take a moment, breathe and just be in the present. Commit to taking the action of meditating a few times a day (which in some circles, is clearly seen as non-action, so there's a lovely spiritual paradox in this one). Take little steps toward this and you will change your future.

Success Strategy Read aloud *Chapter 11: Acting in a Certain Way* from *The Science of Getting Rich* by Wallace D. Wattles. (If you feel you really want to integrate this chapter then find an accountability partner and read it for 30 days. If you miss a day, then start all over again until you do thirty days in a row.) Each night write out six items you intend to do the next day. Prioritize your list and always do the most important ones first. Get into the habit of always finishing this list.

Resources *The Seven Spiritual Laws of Success by Deepak Chopra*
  The Isaiah Effect: Decoding the Lost Science of Prayer and Prophecy by
    Gregg Braden
  Feel The Fear And Do It Anyway by Susan Jeffers
  Prosperity Plus...A New Way of Living by Mary Morrissey

Day 25: The Law Of Gratitude

The Law: Spiritual currency magnetizes abundance to you. Gratitude is the feeling in harmony with abundance.

> *"Gratitude is the sign of noble souls."*
> Aesop

My Personal Illustration

Every day I write in my gratitude journal, even if they are only "tiny" things. You might laugh, but I am so grateful every morning in my shower for hot water. Sometimes just using the Law of Relativity, I am ever so grateful for all that we have in this part of the world. I feel very blessed to live in Canada and have the luxuries that we have here.

You see gratitude in the suggested applications for the 30 Day Plan. I have also explored a program developed by Shawn Achor, the author of *"The Happiness Advantage: Linking Positive Brains to Performance."* This program includes, among other activities, finding three new things I am grateful for each day just as we do in the 30 Day Plan. Following the program is supposed to bring more happiness into your life, and so far it feels really good to do all of these things. The clever thing about this program is that when it is followed, it is a vibration changer (there's that Law of Vibration again).

In business the higher your vibration, the stronger your success.

Your Reading Meditation for The Law Of Gratitude

This meditation is a key to unlocking your soul's inner knowing about this Universal Law. It is already in you, so use this time to bring it to your conscious understanding. Read the following meditation slowly.

Take a nice deep breath in through your nose and let it out through your mouth. You are going to let all the tension leave your body, and as you exhale, repeat in your mind the word: Relax.

You are in the right place at the right time. Your body and mind are in a highly creative vibration right now. Your mind and your heart are ready to receive whatever it is that you need to know. You have the best possible guidance to allow you to experience the teachings of this Law, and to gather all the important information in any way that it appears.

Gratitude is in harmony with abundance and is closely aligned with the Law of Attraction. With the Law of Gratitude, being thankful for what you already have, makes you realize just how wonderfully blessed you are.

The more grateful and consciously appreciative you are of what you have can amplify blessings and abundance into your life. Being grateful for aspects of your life will also rouse the sense of great delight. More conscious people give thanks for what most people ordinarily take for granted. Those expressing appreciation of life are generally more willing to exercise, less depressed, and live life fully. When you're feeling grateful for what you currently have, rather than dwelling on what you don't yet have, you will deal much better with the little hiccups in life. When you feel gratitude, those negative feelings—anger, fear, despair, hatred, and so on—lessen and disappear. The positive will always dispel the negative. When you are grateful for what you already have, then the universe will manifest many more good things into your life.

Another technique using this Law occurs when you "give thanks in advance" for what you want to occur. You feel the gratitude while seeing your visualization as if you have already received it. Doing so, you are transmitting very powerful signals out into the universe. This speeds up the process of manifesting what you want to be, have or do.

Being in gratitude puts you closer to the Universal Intelligence or God energy. Living in gratitude is working in harmony with the other Laws of the Universe. Gratitude is very powerful—it is spiritual currency. It will increase your faith and your happiness. It is a very high-energy positive vibration of thought, which acts like a magnet. The entire process of receiving on the mental, spiritual and material planes can be summed up as being in a state of gratitude.

Imagine saying and REALLY feeling: For this day, I am grateful.

Now, to finish your reading, take three deep cleansing breaths, knowing that with each breath you integrate the information you have received. Trust that this is so, and it will be.

Suggested Applications for Today's Law of Flow

Meditate Use the meditation provided for this Law by finding a quiet place to read the selection, or you can listen to the recording of it (if you have purchased the mp3's that go with this book), or use another meditation that appeals to you. (At least 15 minutes)

Gratitude Write at least three things that you are grateful for on this magnificent day. Connect to the feeling of gratitude.

Exercise As you exercise today, thank your body for its strength, flexibility, and stamina and commit to making healthy choices that continue to nourish it. A suggested affirmation is–I give thanks for and honor the miracle that is my body.

Hydrate Drink ½ ounce of pure water per pound of body weight (or 30 ml per kg). 2 glasses upon rising, 2 glasses between breakfast and lunch, 2 glasses between lunch and dinner and 2 after dinner.

Life Insight Find someone you can thank for something, in person. If you can't do it today, arrange to do it as soon as possible!

Mindful Practice Take a moment, breathe and just be in the present. As you prepare to meditate today, silently thank the circle of life that surrounds you. "I see the world with new eyes today, and I am profoundly grateful for my close relationships and the Earth that supports me."

Success Strategy Write out *Chapter 7: Gratitude* from *The Science of Getting Rich* by Wallace D. Wattles. (If you feel you really want to integrate this chapter then find an accountability partner and write it out for 30 days. If you miss a day, then start all over again until you do thirty days in a row.) Send some thank you cards to current customers.

Resources *The Science of Getting Rich Chapter 7* by Wallace D. Wattles
The Secret Gratitude Book by Rhonda Byrne
A Course in Miracles by Foundation for Inner Peace

Day 26: The Law Of Allowing

The Law: The first part of the Law says that you must learn to receive or allow good energy to flow into your life with no resistance. The second part of this Law is allowing others to be who they are.

"For it is in giving that we receive."
St. Francis of Assisi

My Personal Illustration

I have no trouble with the giving part of this Law, since I am a natural giver. But when it comes to the allowing and receiving, well…let's just say that I am still working on that part! I let go for little periods of time and then my control part takes over again. So I am dancing with this one and have not totally surrendered yet. But here's how I'm practicing: in my business, I am letting go of tasks that in the past I thought I had to do (receiving good energy by allowing others to do what they are good at). In my personal life, I am arranging for weekly massages (receiving) and learning to say "No" more often (maintaining good energy by honoring my boundaries). With all my relationships, I am working on allowing everyone I come in contact with to be who they are without any interference on my part. Again, this is a very challenging Law as it is not always easy to do, but the awareness of this Law helps in the process. In my spiritual life, I am paying attention more to the clues and whispers of the universe and allowing the universe to unfold as it will.

Meditation for The Law Of Allowing

This meditation is a key to unlocking your soul's inner knowing about this Universal Law. It is already in you, so use this time to bring it to your conscious understanding. Read the following meditation slowly.

Take a nice deep breath in through your nose and let it out through your mouth. You are going to let all the tension leave your body, and as you exhale, repeat in your mind the word: Relax.

You are in the right place at the right time. Your body and mind are in a highly creative vibration right now. Your mind and your heart are

ready to receive whatever it is that you need to know. You have the best possible guidance to allow you to experience the teachings of this Law, and to gather all the important information in any way that it appears.

> *The Law of Allowing is based on the principle of least action and is applied in two ways. The first way says that you must allow or receive from the Universe and allow good energy including prayer to flow into your life. The second way would be allowing others to be themselves. Even though it could be challenging in relationships, allow people to express with no resistance on your part. This will free up tremendous energy and you will feel real freedom.*
>
> *The universe operates through an energetic exchange of giving and receiving. When you give or offer your intention with no resistance (no negative vibrations) then the energy exchange is to receive or allow.*
>
> *The Law of Allowing will work for you if you let it. What you must accept is that you are worthy to receive. It is OK to just be, let go and allow and embrace a heightened level of consciousness, a guidance. This state of being enables you to powerfully and passionately focus on the Law of Allowing and enable the process of manifestation.*
>
> *When you use your thoughts to manifest something in your life, you are telling the universe what you desire and you feel it in your soul. Amplify your intention with your feelings and emotions. Send out the signal through your vibration to the universe that you are in harmony with what you desire. Then, to complete the cycle of energy flow, allow the result to occur for you, receive it. The universe hears you and supplies you with your intention. Your wish is its command and you get your desired outcome when you are in the right state of consciousness. Just intend it and allow it. Tune into the dynamic exchange of the universe and receive the blessings.*

Now, to finish your reading, take three deep cleansing breaths, knowing that with each breath you integrate the information you have received. Trust that this is so, and it will be.

Suggested Applications for Today's Law of Flow

Meditate Use the meditation provided for this Law by finding a quiet place to read the selection, or you can listen to the recording of it (if you have purchased the mp3's that go with this book), or use another meditation that appeals to you. (At least 15 minutes)

Gratitude Write at least three things that you are grateful for on this magnificent day. Connect to the feeling of gratitude.

Exercise As you exercise, repeat the statement, "Today, I accept everything as it IS." over and over.

Hydrate Drink ½ ounce of pure water per pound of body weight (or 30 ml per kg). 2 glasses upon rising, 2 glasses between breakfast and lunch, 2 glasses between lunch and dinner and 2 after dinner.

Life Insight Practice acceptance. Accept things as they are this moment, not as you wish they were. Accept people as they are, not as you wish they were.

Mindful Practice Take a moment, breathe and just be in the present. Practice non-judgment. Begin your day with the statement, "Today, I shall judge nothing that occurs," and throughout the day remind yourself not to judge. You can also choose to change the meaning of each occurrence.

Success Strategy Create a Mastermind in your mind. It can consist of anywhere between 5 to 10 people (living or dead) who most inspire you. Choose people who represent different aspects of your business. Take at least 15 minutes of quiet time and "call a meeting." Now close your eyes and mentally invite each of "your" Mastermind members to appear in your board room. Ask your question especially about what you are currently working on and then patiently wait for your answer. Take notes and allow and be "open" to all answers.

Resources *The Book of Secrets: Unlocking the Hidden Dimensions of Your Life* by Deepak Chopra

Law of Attraction: The Science of Attracting More of What You Want and Less of What You Don't by Michael J. Losier

The Law of Attraction: How to Make It Work for You by Esther Hicks, Jerry Hicks

The Law of Receiving from Raymond Holliwell's *Working With The Law*

Letting Go: The Pathway of Surrender by David R. Hawkins

Day 27: The Law Of Manifestation

The Law: Wherever you place your attention the universe interprets as your intention. You are manifesting all the time—you just aren't always aware of this process.

> *"There are qualities one must possess to win— definiteness of purpose, the knowledge of what one wants, and a burning desire to possess it."*
> Napoleon Hill

My Personal Illustration

When I decided to manifest my first book, I did so because people wanted more help with understanding their health, specifically their immune system. So my intention was to fulfill a need I observed. I had never written anything before and I did not even type! So in the beginning it was a real fantasy, but my goal was to write a book about the immune system that the layperson could easily understand.

I started writing and researching, but also began my manifestation practice at the same time

Every day, I visualized the book completed and having a launch party. (Whenever I had doubts, I replaced those thoughts by visualizing different phases of completion in different ways.)

I felt the excitement of being able to show off my new creation (it was similar to having another baby).

All the while I was consistently working on the book. I produced a new chapter every two weeks. (Manifestation always needs an element of action…see Day 24: The Law of Action.)

I participated in a Mastermind program that made me accountable to others. The accountability helped especially when I was nearly done, and started to get tired of my writing and wanted a change. (That was probably an old paradigm trying to prevent my completion.)

I renewed my intention many times to keep myself going, especially near the end, because that was when lots of obstacles reared their heads. Many times I almost talked myself out of finishing, but thanks to the daily affirmations, the support, and the firm commitment I had made, I kept going. The bestselling book "The Immune System Handbook" became a reality.

In business, using this Law is essential. It is important to be conscious of what you desire to manifest, otherwise you will feel like life is happening TO you instead of THROUGH you.

Meditation for The Law Of Manifestation

This meditation is a key to unlocking your soul's inner knowing about this Universal Law. It is already in you, so use this time to bring it to your conscious understanding. Read the following meditation slowly.

Take a nice deep breath in through your nose and let it out through your mouth. You are going to let all the tension leave your body, and as you exhale, repeat in your mind the word: Relax.

You are in the right place at the right time. Your body and mind are in a highly creative vibration right now. Your mind and your heart are ready to receive whatever it is that you need to know. You have the best possible guidance to allow you to experience the teachings of this Law, and to gather all the important information in any way that it appears.

Manifestation is brought about by both attention and intention. Where you place your attention, the universe hears as your intention. You are manifesting all the time, but you just aren't aware of this process. As you know, whenever you do not choose your thoughts, you are creating by default.

So the question is, what do you really want? Take the blinders off your mind and totally engage your imagination. Just remember: If it is a really worthy goal or manifestation, it is going to encourage you to grow and develop your potential. Also it must be something you fully desire and intent, be in agreement with your inner core values and be totally clear. It is essential to be in alignment with your purpose, good for others and in harmony with all that is.

Stay focused on your worthy goal and how you are going to feel once you attain it. Fall in love with it. Once you have written down and launched your goal, you must then look forward to it, not with hope, but with perfect knowing that it will happen. Welcome it as already accomplished. Through the aid of your five senses and your imagination you must form a specific, clear, concise image of yourself having achieved your goal. This helps develop synapses of cells of recognition in your brain. Place your written goal wherever you can view it daily. Be committed to the vision of your goal but be flexible in the process.

If you think you have contradictory thoughts about your goal then, stop, relax and visualize again. Do this until you feel excited about your manifestation actually being fulfilled. Let go, allow and feel the gratitude for the goal already being manifested. Once your goal appears in your world exactly as you imagined it, you have completed your manifestation. Thank the infinite Universe and then accept it into your life.

Now, to finish your reading, take three deep cleansing breaths, knowing that with each breath you integrate the information you have received. Trust that this is so, and it will be.

Suggested Applications for Today's Law of Flow

Meditate Use the meditation provided for this Law by finding a quiet place to read the selection, or you can listen to the recording of it (if you have purchased the mp3's that go with this book), or use another meditation that appeals to you. (At least 15 minutes)

Gratitude Write at least three things that you are grateful for on this magnificent day. Connect to the feeling of gratitude.

Exercise Focus on your health goals. See only those final states of strength, shape, endurance, and ability.

Hydrate Drink ½ ounce of pure water per pound of body weight (or 30 ml per kg). 2 glasses upon rising, 2 glasses between breakfast and lunch, 2 glasses between lunch and dinner and 2 after dinner.

Life Insight Commit to writing your intentions on a goal card, and know your outcome. Be passionate and totally committed to your goal. Clarity is power. Carry this goal card with you wherever you go. Look at it before you go into your silence and meditation. Look at it before you go to sleep at night. Look at it when you wake up in the morning. Then, watch how it manifests into your life.

Mindful Practice Take a moment, breathe and just be in the present. See yourself in possession of your desires. Know that they already exist. Have faith in what you are manifesting. See it as if it is already in its physical form. Know that it is so.

Success Strategy Read aloud or write out *Six Ways to Turn Desires Into Gold* from Chapter Two *Desire–The Starting Point of All Achievement–The First Step Toward Riches* from *Think and Grow Rich* by Napoleon Hill. (If you really want to integrate this on your own or with an accountability partner, write it out for 30 days. If you miss a day, start all over again until you do thirty days in a row.)

Resources *Ask and It Is Given* by Esther and Jerry Hicks

Law of Attraction: The Science of Attracting More of What You Want and Less of What You Don't by Michael J. Losier

Life Lessons for Mastering the Law of Attraction: 7 Essential Ingredients for Living a Prosperous Life by Jack Canfield, Mark Victor Hansen

Wishes Fulfilled: Mastering the Art of Manifesting by Wayne W. Dyer

Day 28: The Law Of Compensation

The Law: Compensation is the visible effect of your deeds.

"The only gift is a portion of thyself."
Ralph Waldo Emerson

My Personal Illustration

Money is so misunderstood in our world and I had a lot of learning to do around it too. When I finally understood it, I saw the correlation between my giving value to others and my compensation. Another component was my passion. I noticed that whenever I was passionate about what I was creating, my income rose.

A while back, I was in the path of a stolen car racing down the highway, and was injured when the stolen car hit mine. My passion for doing business was very low during the healing process and my some of my income streams went down. Obviously my vibration was not in a good place and since everything is energy, the universe responded to that vibration. Once I turned that vibration around and regained passion for serving once again, my income went back up.

I have become very aware how all the Laws work together, especially with the Law of Compensation.

Meditation for The Law Of Compensation

This meditation is a key to unlocking your soul's inner knowing about this Universal Law. It is already in you, so use this time to bring it to your conscious understanding. Read the following meditation slowly.

Take a nice deep breath in through your nose and let it out through your mouth. You are going to let all the tension leave your body, and as you exhale, repeat in your mind the word: Relax.

You are in the right place at the right time. Your body and mind are in a highly creative vibration right now. Your mind and your heart are ready to receive whatever it is that you need to know. You have the best possible guidance to allow you to experience the teachings of this Law, and to gather all the important information in any way that it appears.

You've heard the adage "what goes around, comes around." Compensation is the visible effects of your deeds; it can show up as gifts, money, friendships, good health or any other blessing given to you due to your actions.

In the marketplace, the Law Of Compensation pays for value. If you increase your skill (and thereby your value to others), you will increase your income. As Bob Proctor says, "The amount of money you will earn will always be in exact ratio to the need for what you do, your ability to do it, and the difficulty there is to replace you". If you want to increase your compensation, you must amplify the value of your contribution. Your compensation will always be in direct proportion to your service to others.

Your mental attitude, as well as your feelings of happiness and fulfillment, are also the result of the things that you have put into your own mind. Fill your own mind with happy thoughts, full of optimism and dreams of future success, and you will be compensated by those positive experiences in your daily activities. Currency also uses this Law. The more you tap into the infinite supply, and the more you give, the more that will flow back to you.

There is a variation on this which is called The Law of Overcompensation, which states that great success comes from those who always make it a habit to give more than they take. They do more than they are compensated for, go the extra mile, and always look for the opportunity to exceed expectations. Because they are always overcompensating, they are always receiving ample rewards.

To get the most out of relationships with your friends, partnerships, marriage and certainly in business and wealth creation, it is best to give more than you take. In any relationship, or any task in your life, if you want more return, put more positive energy into it. You will be compensated for your good deeds. Give your heart and soul to everything.

Take a moment to feel the abundance and blessings that are coming into your life and connect to the value you are contributing.

Now, to finish your reading, take three deep cleansing breaths, knowing that with each breath you integrate the information you have received. Trust that this is so, and it will be.

Suggested Applications for Today's Law of Flow

Meditate Use the meditation provided for this Law by finding a quiet place to read the selection, or you can listen to the recording of it (if you have purchased the mp3's that go with this book), or use another meditation that appeals to you. (At least 15 minutes)

Gratitude Write at least three things that you are grateful for on this magnificent day. Connect to the feeling of gratitude.

Exercise As you exercise ask yourself, "How can I serve my body today?"

Hydrate Drink ½ ounce of pure water per pound of body weight (or 30 ml per kg). 2 glasses upon rising, 2 glasses between breakfast and lunch, 2 glasses between lunch and dinner and 2 after dinner.

Life Insight Ask yourself throughout your day, "How can I serve with love?" and "How can I help?" Get really good at the service you render.

Mindful Practice Take a moment, breathe and just be in the present. Look at this definition of **MONEY**: **M**y **O**wn **N**atural **E**nergy **Y**ield. (From *The Abundance Book* by John Randolph Price.) Contemplate these words: You are your own money. Money is the physical manifestation of who you are (or who you vibrate). Look at money as the currency of life and be aware of what it is teaching you. Remember to give value and you will be rewarded.

Success Strategy Find *The Abundance Book* by John Randolph Price. Find the Ten Statements of Principle and write them out or speak them out loud. (If you really want to integrate them on your own or with an accountability partner, write them out for 30 days. If you miss a day, then start all over again until you do 30 days in a row.) Spend your money only on things that will propel your dream. Create a new relationship with money.

Resources *The Law of Divine Compensation: On Work, Money, and Miracles* by Marianne Williamson

Busting Loose from the Money Game: Mind-Blowing Strategies for Changing the Rules of a Game You Can't Win by Robert Scheinfeld

You Were Born Rich: Now You Can Discover And Develop Those Riches by Bob Proctor

The Abundance Book by John Randolph Price

The Law of Compensation from Raymond Holliwell's book *Working With The Law*

Secrets of the Millionaire Mind: Mastering the Inner Game of Wealth by T. Harv Eker

Rich Dad, Poor Dad by Robert T. Kiyosaki

Day 29: The Law Of Success

The Law: Personal advancement and manifesting personal desires are ways to enrich the world. Happiness in service is a key component of your success.

> *"Success in life depends upon happiness, and happiness is found in no other way than through service that is rendered in a spirit of love."*
> Napoleon Hill

My Personal Illustration

When I look over my life, I see many successes. I see them in my schooling, my various businesses, my family life, my hobbies, my health, my ability to help others, my friendships, my self-expression, my personal development, my spirituality…so many areas of my life. I must say, though, that learning about this Law and its components made it easier to be successful. When I learned to align myself with the universal energies of expansion and fuller expression, I felt happier overall, and success came easier. When I became aware of the best possible way for me to serve and make a difference in the world, I felt successful.

Again it is clear that there are many kinds of successes. As an entrepreneur, it is important to have successes in many areas of your life, not just work.

Meditation for The Law Of Success

This meditation is a key to unlocking your soul's inner knowing about this Universal Law. It is already in you, so use this time to bring it to your conscious understanding. Read the following meditation slowly.

Take a nice deep breath in through your nose and let it out through your mouth. You are going to let all the tension leave your body, and as you exhale, repeat in your mind the word: Relax.

You are in the right place at the right time. Your body and mind are in a highly creative vibration right now. Your mind and your heart are

ready to receive whatever it is that you need to know. You have the best possible guidance to allow you to experience the teachings of this Law, and to gather all the important information in any way that it appears.

The Universal Law of Success intends that every individual will be supported to become successful and remarkable. Success comes down to personal advancement and manifesting what one desires with intent. However, ultimate success comes when your results benefit your fellow human beings and the world is enriched. Advancement in all areas is the highest purpose of the Law of Success. Persistent adherence to this Law will produce results every time. You may need to change your mileposts occasionally, but never let go of the goal.

Your creative intellectual faculties, when properly developed and scientifically applied, will insure success. To develop your higher faculties into remarkable talents leading to superior knowledge, insight and greater power, you will be required to study, plan, and expend effort along with having faith and understanding. Learning to use two valuable things—your time and your higher thought faculties—are vital skills for success.

If you fail to move forward, you will be prodded until you are in forward motion again. The universe is always moving towards fuller expansion and expression. If you come up against obstacles, you will find that they can draw you out and make you stronger. You can start to view them as stepping-stones to your success. You can see how you can learn from your own failures and by the failures of other people. You can begin to develop new strategies.

Develop a positive mental successful attitude and proceed to think, live, and act with that strong conviction, declaring to yourself the words, "I can." This conviction sets up an optimistic vibration and people are attracted to you and want to do business with you. Every mind can develop greatness and mastery. Become excellent at what you do.

Remember the power is within you when you are connected with the infinite power. There are no limits to your possibilities.

Now, to finish your reading, take three deep cleansing breaths, knowing that with each breath you integrate the information you have received. Trust that this is so, and it will be.

Suggested Applications for Today's Law of Flow

Meditate Use the meditation provided for this Law by finding a quiet place to read the selection, or you can listen to the recording of it (if you have purchased the mp3's that go with this book), or use another meditation that appeals to you. (At least 15 minutes)

Gratitude Write at least three things that you are grateful for on this magnificent day. Connect to the feeling of gratitude.

Exercise See if you can express happiness as you exercise. How happy can you be as you move your body, strengthen yourself, or go longer or faster?

Hydrate Drink ½ ounce of pure water per pound of body weight (or 30 ml per kg). 2 glasses upon rising, 2 glasses between breakfast and lunch, 2 glasses between lunch and dinner and 2 after dinner.

Life Insight Develop your happiness factor. How can you tap into what makes you happy to bring you greater success right now? (Not success sometime later, but NOW...today.)

Mindful Practice Take a moment, breathe and just be in the present. Set aside time today to be totally free to express yourself. Find a quiet space, gather the tools you need, and just enjoy what happens. Notice how you feel after you've spent some time doing what you love. Feel the passion, ease, and the connection with the energy flow.

Success Strategy Be persistent and determined. Read aloud Chapter Nine on *Persistence–The Sustained Effort Necessary to Induce Faith–The Eighth Step Toward Riches* from Think and Grow Rich by Napoleon Hill. (If you really want to integrate this then find an accountability partner and read it out for 30 days. If you miss a day, then start all over again until you do 30 days in a row.) Remember to include success in all areas of your life. Look around you and recognize and acknowledge yourself for all your little successes.

Resources *The Seven Spiritual Laws of Success* by Deepak Chopra

The Law of Success from Raymond Holliwell's book *Working With The Law*

You 2: A High Velocity Formula for Multiplying Your Personal Effectiveness in Quantum Leaps by Price Pritchett

The Success Principles: How to Get from Where You Are to Where You Want to Be by Jack Canfield and Janet Switzer

Day 30: The Law Of Masterminding

The Law: There is a synergy that occurs between like-minded individuals gathered together to create success and tap into the ultimate Master Mind.

*"You CAN NOT achieve your major definite purpose in
life without using the power of the MasterMind."*
Napoleon Hill

My Personal Illustration

Masterminding has been an essential part of my growth. When I am in a Mastermind, my Mastermind partners hold me accountable, they support me, and they believe in me (even when I don't). They hold up my dreams, they bring in other perspectives, they show me new possibilities I may not have thought of before, and they strengthen me.

I credit my first Mastermind with helping me stay with my first book to completion. Through this process, I saw that it was much easier to create something when supported. The other aspect of this Law is accessing the Master Mind, the Universal Spirit. Once I do that, I feel I am in the flow—I then have access to All That Is. That is my wish for you as well.

Meditation for The Law Of Masterminding

This meditation is a key to unlocking your soul's inner knowing about this Universal Law. It is already in you, so use this time to bring it to your conscious understanding. Read the following meditation slowly.

Take a nice deep breath in through your nose and let it out through your mouth. You are going to let all the tension leave your body, and as you exhale, repeat in your mind the word: Relax.

You are in the right place at the right time. Your body and mind are in a highly creative vibration right now. Your mind and your heart are ready to receive whatever it is that you need to know. You have the best possible guidance to allow you to experience the teachings of this Law, and to gather all the important information in any way that it appears.

Although mastermind groups have been around since the beginning of time, the concept of the "mastermind alliance" was formally introduced by Dr. Napoleon Hill in his timeless classic, "Think And Grow Rich."

Dr. Hill defines it "as a mind that is developed through the harmonious cooperation of two or more people who ally themselves for the purpose of accomplishing any given task." Hill uses ideas from physics to illustrate the synergy that occurs between like-minded individuals. Another key insight from Hill is that knowledge is not power–it is only potential power. He defines power as "...organized knowledge, expressed through intelligent efforts." The mastermind group makes this materialize.

Mastermind groups offer a combination of peer accountability, brainstorming, education and support in a group setting to sharpen your personal and business skills. A mastermind group helps you, along with your mastermind group members, to achieve success. You create a community of committed, supportive colleagues who brainstorm together to move the members to new heights. Remember you become who and what you surround yourself with, so choosing the right Mastermind partners is crucial for success.

Participants challenge each other to set important goals and follow through to accomplish them. The group requires confidentiality, commitment, creativity and brainstorming ideas/solutions, supporting each other with total honesty, respect, co-operation and compassion. Mastermind group members act as devil's advocates, supportive colleagues, and catalysts for growth.

Since everyone in a Mastermind group will bring something different to the table, the process will strengthen your experience and knowledge. No individual has ever really achieved success without the help and cooperation of others. Working together with like-minded individuals brings out the best in each other and allows the opportunity to bounce ideas off each other as well.

All successful people have worked with a team of individuals who were all working towards achieving the same objective in their respective companies. It doesn't matter how small or big your alliance is, but the important thing to remember is to align yourself with others who are positive, self-motivated, goal-oriented and driven to succeed.

Napoleon Hill said, "No two minds ever come together without thereby creating a third, invisible intangible force, which may be likened to a third mind (the Master Mind)." The highest purpose of a Mastermind group is to establish a conscious contact with the Universal Mind, and for all members to experience an increased awareness and higher level of consciousness, knowing that the Mastermind is working in and through them.

Now, to finish your reading, take three deep cleansing breaths, knowing that with each breath you integrate the information you have received. Trust that this is so, and it will be.

Suggested Applications for Today's Law of Flow

Meditate Use the meditation provided for this Law by finding a quiet place to read the selection, or you can listen to the recording of it (if you have purchased the mp3's that go with this book), or use another meditation that appeals to you. (At least 15 minutes)

Gratitude Write at least three things that you are grateful for on this magnificent day. Connect to the feeling of gratitude.

Exercise If you have a local Mastermind group, see if you can exercise with all or some of the members today. If your Mastermind is not local, find someone you can exercise with today.

Hydrate Drink ½ ounce of pure water per pound of body weight (or 30 ml per kg). 2 glasses upon rising, 2 glasses between breakfast and lunch, 2 glasses between lunch and dinner and 2 after dinner.

Life Insight Find a group of like-minded people who all want to create a new future. When you have found the right individuals, form your own Mastermind group.

Mindful Practice Take a moment, breathe and just be in the present. Go into meditation today with the intention of getting in touch with the ultimate Master Mind: Universal Spirit/The Divine/Source/God/ The "I Am."

Success Strategy In your Mastermind group, make sure each member makes a contribution in alignment with their own expertise. Everyone has a significant role to play in each member's success. Surround yourself with successful people and share your dream. If you don't currently have a physical Mastermind group see the success strategy from Day 26 The Law of Allowing.

Resources *The Law of Success In Sixteen Lessons* by Napoleon Hill

Think and Grow Rich Napoleon Hill

You Were Born Rich: Now You Can Discover and Develop Those Riches by Bob Proctor

Meet and Grow Rich: How to Easily Create and Operate Your Own "Mastermind" Group for Health, Wealth, and More by Joe Vitale and Bill Hibbler

The Quantum of Flow

*"Everything we call real is made of things that cannot be
regarded as real. If quantum mechanics hasn't profoundly
shocked you, you haven't understood it yet."*
Niels Bohr

When I first read the above quote, it triggered my inquisitive
nature. I just had to know more, so I began to delve more
deeply into the area of quantum physics. In my endless search to see how
"all of this" works, I found that in the quantum world, things started to
come together for me.

Now, I understand that many people are scared off because of the
word "physics." I know it might even take them back to memories of
high school physics, which was not everyone's cup of tea. I failed that
course in school myself! So let's let the old associations with that word
go and explore this new territory as adults with plenty of life experience.
That life experience is going to come in handy to help explore the implications of what this wonderful realm has to offer.

Quantum physics is exciting; it takes us into the unseen and undiscov-
ered. Personally, it helps me understand this world through the lens of my
level of awareness, whatever level that might be on any particular day.

Everything in our lives, in the entire world, in fact, is the result of our
consciousness or awareness as it stands now. Our lives will unfold
perfectly and precisely just as we "believe" that it will–in fact our lives
are as they are now because of what we believe about ourselves and what
we think of ourselves. Based on years of practice with this, whenever I
place a new set of belief systems or thoughts or awareness within me, I
watch how the world changes as my consciousness has changed. For

instance, when I changed my belief around owning a house, the right house appeared. When I go into a state of profound gratitude, my whole world is bright and beautiful, and all kinds of wonderful occurrences happen for me that I would never have predicted. When I focus on the present moment, all my activities are orchestrated with perfect timing.

Try it yourself, take a moment and just concentrate on the present moment and breathe. You will notice it is just your consciousness on your breath in that moment in space and time. Your cares and worries have no place there.

Remember every one of your thoughts, words, feelings and actions are all forms of energy. Even the thoughts, words and feelings housed in your subconscious mind. What you think, say, feel and do in each moment creates your reality. The combined thoughts, words, feelings and actions of everyone on the planet creates our collective consciousness, and that collective consciousness creates the world you see before us.

Now let's turn to the quantum world and see it from another angle.

We all have been conditioned into an old model of reality: cause and effect using just our five senses. That is, we wait for something outside of us to happen so we can feel differently inside, and when we feel different we pay attention to what caused it. But let's look at the quantum version: quantum physics goes beyond the senses. It is nonsense, or non-sense. Reality here exists *beyond* the senses. Quantum physics is revolutionizing the way we "see" things. It is showing us that everything is energy.

That one concept alone is a profound shift from the age-old idea from Newtonian physics that the world is solid matter and behaves like a machine. Since we were all schooled around this idea of solid and separateness, it may be challenging to grasp a new concept such as this one. But stay with me here, and you'll see the profound implications of it.

What quantum physicists like Max Planck, Werner Heisenberg, and Niels Bohr are saying is that everything is made up of waves of infinite potential and these waves are everywhere. The quantum field is an "infinite" field of potential. Everything in the entire cosmos is nothing but a huge vibrating ball of interrelated infinite energy, which has the ability to interconnect into infinity with no regard to space and time. Our individual thought (consciousness) is the key to triggering the energy to form whatever we are imagining.

On the quantum level, energy begins as a wave and as it is observed, it transmutes into a particle and joins with additional particles that harmonize with its frequency. Energy (waves) respond to, transmute and appear as particles (solid objects) based on our thoughts. Another way to say this is, anything and everything that exists in our world once existed as a wave (spiritual, unseen realm) and through individual observation and expectation (thoughts, values, assumptions and beliefs) it is transformed into a particle (made physical).

In other words, the energy begins taking form immediately based on your thoughts and beliefs. Thoughts, which are determined by your beliefs, values, expectations or assumptions, are broadcast outward into the infinite field of "wave" energy much like a radio frequency, transformed from waves (spiritual realm) to particles (matter) and join together with additional energies which vibrate at a harmonious frequency and combine to shape what you come to see as your life experience in the physical world—your physical world! You quite literally have the ability to mold and shape the various areas of your life, based on your thoughts, beliefs, values, expectations, assumptions and feelings either consciously or subconsciously.

The thoughts that you think are the *electrical* charge in the quantum field, the feelings that you emote are the *magnetic* charge in the quantum field. How you think and how you feel broadcasts an electro-magnetic signal that influences every single atom in your life. The thought sends the signal out and the feeling draws the event back. So ask yourself, what are you broadcasting every day? Whatever you are broadcasting, you are messaging the quantum field. The quantum field is an objective field, it exists beyond time and space, it is both personal and universal, it is within you and all around you and is highly responsive to how you think and how you feel. So if you are broadcasting a feeling into the field consciously or subconsciously what you are really saying is, I want to experience this event equal to whom I am *being* in consciousness expressed through this feeling.

Energy and matter are two sides of the same coin. Our thoughts (which are also energy) are like switching stations. They can take the waves or unseen energy and make the subatomic particles show up physically (matter). So we are very creative beings. Quantum physics tells us that it is the act of observing an object (events, results, conditions and circumstances) that causes it to be there and the outcome is based only on how we observe it. So unless there is an observer there is no existing object. Events, results, conditions and circumstances cannot exist independent of its observer.

Also remember that the quantum physicists are saying that these waves exist potentially everywhere and they call that "superlocation"–everything is potentially in more than one place simultaneously. So everything is potentially everywhere. (Hard to grasp, I know.)

To understand this concept, look at radio waves. These waves are everywhere and bounce around the world. We choose to tune into a particular frequency through the "channel" we select. That way we are personalizing that frequency with the one we chose. We can choose to tune into frequencies of depression or joy.

Thanks to quantum physics it is clear that you are quite literally the creator of your reality! You, as the producer and director of your movie, are responsible for whatever is occurring in your life right now. If you desire to change the events, results, conditions, and circumstances in your life, you only need change the thoughts, beliefs, values, assumptions and vibrations (emotions) that are responsible for them forming your reality through your level of consciousness or awareness.

So what happens if we unconsciously create by using frozen patterns (paradigms) of information that we have memorized from the past?

With awareness, energy begins taking form immediately based on our thoughts and beliefs. Whatever you think about and believe to be true (regardless of whether or not those beliefs or assumptions are based on "real truth" or "perceived truth"), acts in exact accordance to the way that it is "believed" and this determines how your life will unfold. (You can now see how important it is to undo any limiting thinking patterns, values, paradigms or belief systems and replace them with new ones that serve you.)

Quantum reality says mind and matter are comingled, and that our subjective mind has an effect on the objective world. When we look (are aware), the waves of energy collapse into a quantum event. The moment we take our attention off the atom, it goes back into energy. So if we are observing our reality from the same level of mind and emotion of the past, then that is causing us to see our future through the lens of the past. Our quantum observation is keeping those same patterns of possibility collapsed into the same reality called our life–frozen into the same patterns of information.

What emotions have you memorized that have become part of your identity? (Guilt, fear, low self-worth?) What images do you believe about yourself that aren't really who you are, but are simply a residue from your past images? (A bad parent, a failure, not good enough, lazy?)

As you become more conscious of your unconscious self (your subconscious mind), you have more control over it. You begin to free your body from the locked emotional state and release energy because you are opening up to "all possibilities". When you free your body from the chains of those emotions that keep you connected to the past, then the body relaxes into the present moment (where all the creative potential is).

To shift into a new state of being and connect to future possibilities is actually fairly easy, from the quantum perspective. In the quantum field, infinite waves of possibility collapse into a quantum event called an experience. Every day, as the quantum observer, you observe that creation as you cause particles to coagulate into a reality. When you are in a new state of being (consciousness) with a new intention and elevated emotion, you feel connected to something greater. You feel expanded. With this kind of awareness, you never force or control the outcome. In this state, you have readily available energy with which to create a new future.

You have probably done this many times, and just didn't know it. Whenever you mentally rehearse whom you are going to be ahead of the event, you are reminding yourself of who you want to be. In this creative state you feel connected to something greater, you have reconditioned your body to a new mind, the emotions of survival are transmuted into elevated emotions of joy and gratitude, and your body is beginning to get a taste of what the future reality is in the present moment. In this scenario, you have just moved from living in your past to living in your future.

With repetition, you condition your body to believe it has already happened. This signals new neural pathways, so your body begins to physically change to look like the experience has happened. The emotional signature of gratitude is that it has already happened.

This program is so powerful that your subconscious mind does not know the difference between your imagined reality and current reality. To your body it is exactly the same. You are no longer waiting for the event to happen, you have experienced it already. When you move into that state of being, where the mind and body are altered, just relax... because this is when the event finds YOU.

When you are in a state of being, the quantum field responds to who you are being. Not what you are thinking, not what you are feeling, but who you are BEING. Because your body is already living in the future, it is being drawn to that event. You are broadcasting a whole new set of signals, so your job now is to maintain that modified state your entire day, regardless of what is currently going on in your life. If you can sustain that change with constant repetition, then you had better get ready, because you will experience the life of your dreams (quite literally).

Because Quantum Law says that your environment is a manifestation of your mind, if you truly change your mind, there should be tangible evidence in your life and it should come in a way that you least expect. (Because if you expect it, it is not new; if you can predict it, it is more of the same.) It has to leave you with no doubt that what you did *inside* of you produced a result *outside* of you. (The best use of the Law of Cause and Effect.) And when you pay attention to what you did to get that result, you will be able to do it again and again.

Just think of it—our biggest hopes, dreams and desires, already exist as waves in the quantum field (which holds all possibilities within it). These probabilities are only awaiting our awareness of them, and our focus on them, to bring them into our world. That means that with the power of our thoughts, feelings, words and actions to create the world around us, we have the ability to create a world that The Pachamama Alliance describes as environmentally sustainable, socially just and spiritually fulfilling. In order to do this, it is essential that we learn to take control of our thoughts and emotions and transform them into vibrations that allow the infinite possibilities to unfold.

I hope this exploration of the quantum realm will inspire you to find out more about this way of looking at your world. (There are more specific reading suggestions at the end of this book, too.) There is so much potential and possibility here. Soon you will realize that peace and happiness are in your very nature. And I hope that the new thoughts and habits within the 30 Day Plan will help you to use the 30 Laws of Flow to manifest the world of your dreams. I am going to leave you with a quote from one of my other books, The Privilege.

"What a privilege to experience the transformation
of consciousness.

What a privilege to experience surrender, silence, stillness.

What a privilege to experience oneness.

What a privilege to experience infinite possibility.

What a privilege to experience the immeasurable,
the sacred, the essence.

Thank you for the privilege of this lifetime!"

Now What?

Life is habit. Or rather life is a succession of habits.
Samuel Beckett

Some of you may look at your life and not be happy with what you see. You may look at the ideas in this book as complete fantasy. You may be in debt, experiencing ill health, in unhappy relationships, not clear on your purpose or passions, feeling overwhelmed with negative emotions, and feel generally out of control of your circumstances. You may be asking, why me? What's wrong with me? Why do other people have it so good, and I struggle for everything? (Believe me, I know these questions well because I've had them myself.)

When we view reality from our physical senses, then everything looks bleak because we think our senses show us the whole picture. But from the point of view of quantum physics, the body is only a stream of sensations, perceptions, memories and ideations: in essence, an abstraction. But when we start to understand that we are spiritual beings living in a physical body, then all sorts of possibilities open up. Even debt, ill health, and unhappy relationships can be seen as messengers letting us know that our inner world needs addressing. But that requires a big shift in perception, and there is a lot standing in the way.

What Holds Us Back

- Resistance. Unknowingly, we can stop the natural and beneficial flow of energy with our own vibrational pattern. As you learned from the Law of Attraction, if our vibration is not life-giving, then we will not attract what we say we want.

- Our Self Image. Our performance will never exceed our self-esteem by very much or for very long.
- Old Paradigms. These are beliefs or assumptions that are housed in our subconscious mind. They can be passed on from one generation to the next. When we are not consciously recreating our life, these old patterns, values, behaviors and fixed habits unconsciously create it for us.
- The Past. When our identities are trapped in old beliefs, values, expectations and assumptions, "the way things have always been" can really hold us back from our true potential.
- Focusing Outward. This means spending our time and energy imagining that something material—food, sex, power, fame—is going to make us really happy. The greatest teachers and sages throughout time have said that only the urge to find your real Self can make you truly happy.
- Victim Thinking. We are raised in an environment that breeds a victim mentality. It is everywhere especially in the media. It is important to challenge this pervasive thinking.
- Wanting to be Saved. We are all looking for that magical someone or something to rescue us. This is especially highlighted with the archetype of the knight in shining armor syndrome.
- Not Facing our "Shadow" Side. This refers to an unconscious aspect of our personality which the conscious mind tends to ignore or is unaware of. Generally speaking it acts out "negatively" and usually relates to some aspect of low self-esteem.
- Living a Lie. This refers to a variety of problems, including living someone else's life; listening to everyone else and not our own inner voice; living a repressed life; and accepting the lies that we were told as a youngster.
- Living in a Rut. This is where life has lost its meaning. We haven't questioned anything in a long time and we've been running on old habits, paradigms or patterns for so long, it feels terrifying to do anything new.
- Not Being Present. Always thinking about what is next instead of being in the present.

- Not Honoring the Body. The body is our vehicle while we are here, and how we spend our time, use our energy, and choose our fuel is important to our experience. Being out of balance and scattered does not enhance our experience of living, and it can cause successive experiences to spiral downhill quickly. Self-care is vital to getting different results with our intentions, dreams and goals.
- Not Asking for Help. No one can accomplish any big goal alone, or make any huge change by themselves. Support is always needed, and especially when in unfamiliar territory and moving towards a new horizon.

The list could go on and on; there are as many ways we hold ourselves back as there are individuals. But that's where this book can make a difference.

The 30 Laws of Flow is designed to give you applications that will create new positive habits. It is intended to give you new insights and rituals/habits/practices to create success and to be more aligned with the flow of life. You can anticipate a journey of self-development going through the program. You can do this in a 30 Day plan (highly recommended in three, six and twelve month programs), or create your own timeframe. Repetition is encouraged. You can use it to improve your personal life or you can use the success strategies and apply it to your entrepreneurial ventures magnifying your flow of time, money and productivity.

However you use it, my hope for you as you read this book and practice the meditations, study the Laws, and work with the new insights and habits, is that

- You are reminded what an effective creator you really are.
- You are more aware that you have choices
- You develop the strong belief that you can create the reality of your choice.
- You begin to understand your results are an expression of your level of awareness.
- You increase your level of consciousness and awareness.

- You are able to override old paradigms with new healthy patterns.
- You feel comfortable with your inner world and connect inside daily.
- You begin to activate the vast potential inside of you.
- You begin to realize that you have complete and total control over your thinking, your attitude and your vibration.
- You see that you are responsible for everything that is happening in your world especially from a quantum physics point of view.
- You change your thought patterns to focus on what you truly desire.
- You see how to bring about meaningful and lasting change by integrating these success rituals/habits/practices.
- You work with a coach or Mastermind team or community who believe in you and support you unconditionally, giving you an accurate reflection of your real potential and holding you accountable.

Here's a parable about breaking free of powerful mindsets from my friend Chris O'Connor, a public speaker with a focus on health care. He shared this fable at a recent workshop we were both facilitating

In case you are not familiar with Fruit Loops, they are a cereal in North America. So the story begins inside a cereal box, where Fruit Loops live. But because they are inside the box, they don't even know what they are. It's dark, they are all crowded in and they can't even conceive of a world existing outside; all they see is the inside of their box. They don't realize all the instructions are on the outside of the box.

One day, one of the Fruit Loops escapes through a hole in the top. Outside the familiar container, this Fruit Loop discovers a whole new world and sees his home for what it is: a box. He realizes that it has beautiful decorations on the outside. The markings he sees there tells him "what" he is...a Fruit Loop. He discovers his "worth" through the nutrition information on the side. He learns that if you add this thing called M-I-L-K, Fruit Loops become even MORE nutritious!

Exploring another side of his home, the Fruit Loop discovers wonderful puzzles and games to be solved. And beyond this small box lies an incredibly huge and infinite space that those inside could never comprehend.

Knowing the difficulties in going back and explaining what he has learned, he still decides to try. But on his return, he is amazed to discover that the others don't want to hear about this fantastical world. They don't want to know anything about it at all. They just want the top sealed so they can get back to life as usual.

Enthralled with this new world of possibilities, this lone Fruit Loop knows he can't stay inside the box any longer. He decides to go back out and see if he can find other Fruit Loops who have escaped the old paradigm of "inside the box thinking." He knows he will need help from other explorers like him to avoid getting scared by the new, and getting sucked back into the old mentality.

The moral of the story: sometimes it is hard to break from the "inside the box" mindset, and it is even more difficult to convince those still trapped in it that things can be so much better. The best thing to do is find the other Fruit Loops who "get it"; others who have had the experience of greater possibility, who can share in the enthusiasm of this new way of thinking, and are ready to explore new worlds.

We all need support. To give a personal example, in the writing of this book, I was even more conscious of my incessant mind chatter. It was a constant battle to fend off thoughts like, 'Why are you doing this? There are thousands of other books just like it out there. Who do you think you are anyway?' On and on, day after day, every SINGLE day, I would hear these thoughts, and some days it felt like they were getting the upper hand.

These old paradigms are so strong because they boil down to three main universal fears

- The fear of abandonment/separation
- The fear of not being worthy or good enough or important enough
- The fear of surrendering or trusting

   and for many people, a fourth fear

- The fear of making mistakes and that failure is bad.

In the process of writing this book, I encountered all of these at different times.

These fears show up in so many ways in our lives that we need plenty of continual support to transcend them. *Never* underestimate the power of support. Mastermind groups, business networking groups, and other skill development groups are so effective because they provide consistent education, opportunities to practice, principles that are repeated over and over, and a supportive environment for all to share. The bottom line is no one can do it alone; we all need a cheerleader or a champion and a community of like-minded people to support us on our journeys.

Without encouragement from my support groups, coaches and accountability partners, I would never have been able to resist the endless tirade of old thoughts and paradigms trying to keep things the same. I had to use the principles of all 30 Laws to stay focused on my goal, seeing it as though it was already accomplished even when all the obstacles appeared.

As my visualizations became even more powerful, I envisioned all the people who would benefit from the Going For The Flow programs. I saw a community of people coming together online to support one another to stay focused on their dreams. I envisioned their excitement as they neared their goals. I imagined my own enthusiasm for each individual's accomplishments as they shared stories of the miracles in their lives. As I saw and felt these things, they became more and more real to me, and a compelling idea was born: the *30 Laws of Flow Community.*

As time goes on, the *30 Laws of Flow Community* will be updated with fresh material and additional features but here are some highlights I envision:

- A testimonial victory page supporting your new results
- A private Facebook page
- A Success Habits Tracker
- Weekly conference calls (archived for your convenience)
- Accountability partners to support the process
- Opportunity to meet people and build friendships worldwide with a trusted network of like-minded seekers

- Mutual support and encouragement in a friendly, member web-based forum
- Positive interaction, collaboration, masterminding, and creative synergy for entrepreneurs

Here are some of the support program packages for diving more deeply into the 30 Laws of Flow.

- *Going For The Flow–Discovering the Flow: 3 months of the 30 Day Plan*

- *Going For The Flow–Exploring the Flow: 6 months of the 30 Day Plan*

- *Going For The Flow–Living the Flow: Full Year of the 30 Day Plan*

To find out which program is right for you, go to **www.30Lawsof Flow.com**. As more material is added, more options and features will be developed, so check back often.

I look forward to welcoming you to our community of entrepreneurs, seekers, and adventurers who want to experience the flow every day. I know that extraordinary results will be created, and those results will enrich our communities, our nations, and our planet.

Namaste,
Charlene Day

*You intended to come forth into the physical realm of
contrast to define what is wanted, to connect
with the Energy that creates worlds,
and to flow it toward your objects of attention,
not because the objects of attention are important–
but because the act of flowing is essential to life.*
Abraham (Esther Hicks)

Excerpted from a workshop in Lincroft, NJ on Tuesday, October 15th, 1996

© by Jerry & Esther Hicks, **AbrahamHicks.com** (830) 755-2299.

Suggested Resources

7 Habits of Highly Effective People by Stephen Covey

40 Day Mind Fast Soul Feast: A Guide to Soul Awakening and Inner Fulfillment by Michael Bernard Beckwith

A Course in Miracles by Foundation for Inner Peace

A New Earth: Awakening to Your Life's Purpose by Eckhart Tolle

A Path with Heart: A Guide Through the Perils and Promises of Spiritual Life by Jack Kornfield

A Treatise on Cosmic Fire by Alice A. Bailey

Acres of Diamonds by Russell Conwell

Ageless Body, Timeless Mind: The Quantum Alternative to Growing Old by Deepak Chopra

As A Man Thinketh by James Allen

Ask and It Is Given: Learning to Manifest Your Desires by Esther Hicks

Awaken the Giant Within by Tony Robbins

Awakened Imagination by Neville Goddard

Basic Laws of Cosmic Power by Eric Butterworth

Book of the Law by Aleister Crowley

Breaking the Habit of Being Yourself: How to Love Your Mind and Create a New One by Dr. Joe Dispenza

Buddha's Brain: The Practical Neuroscience of Happiness, Love & Wisdom by Rick Hanson and Richard Mendius

Building Your Field of Dreams by Mary Morrissey

Busting Loose from the Money Game: Mind-Blowing Strategies for Changing the Rules of a Game You Can't Win by Robert Scheinfeld

Change Your Thoughts–Change Your Life: Living the Wisdom of the Tao by Wayne W. Dyer

Conative Connection: Uncovering the Link Between Who You Are and How You Perform by Kathy Kolbe

Dancing Wu Li Masters: An Overview of the New Physics by Gary Zukav

Edinburgh Lectures on Mental Science by Thomas Troward

Entanglement by Gregg Braden

Esoteric Healing: A Treatise On The Seven Rays Volume IV by Alice A. Bailey

Feel The Fear And Do It Anyway by Susan Jeffers

Flow: The Psychology of Optimal Experience by Mihaly Csikszentmihalyi

Fractal Time by Gregg Braden

Good Business: Leadership, Flow, and the Making of Meaning by Mihaly Csik-szentmihalyi

Good to Great by Jim Collins

Heal Your Body by Louise Hay

How To Use Your Power by Ernest Holmes

How to Win Friends and Influence People by Dale Carnegie

Illusions by Richard Bach

In Tune with the Infinite by Ralph Waldo Trine

Influence– the Psychology of Persuasion by Robert B. Cialdini

Law of Attraction: The Science of Attracting More of What You Want and Less of What You Don't by Michael J. Losier

Letting Go: The Pathway of Surrender by David R. Hawkins

Life Lessons for Mastering the Law of Attraction: 7 Essential Ingredients for Living a Prosperous Life by Jack Canfield, Mark Victor Hansen

Life Visioning: A Transformative Process for Activating Your Unique Gifts and Highest Potential by Michael Bernard Beckwith

Manifest Your Destiny by Wayne Dyer

Meet and Grow Rich: How to Easily Create and Operate Your Own "Mastermind" Group for Health, Wealth, and More by Joe Vitale and Bill Hibbler

Money is Love: Some Things are Worth Believing In by Klaus J Joehle

Mystic Words of Mighty Power by Walter DeVoe

No Less Than Greatness by Mary Morrissey

Power of Intention by Dr. Wayne Dyer

Power vs. Force: The Hidden Determinants of Human Behavior by David R. Hawkins

Prosperity Plus …A New Way of Living by Mary Morrissey

Psycho-Cybernetics by Dr. Maxwell Maltz

Psycho Pictography by Vernon Howard

Purple Cow by Seth Godin

Quantum Physics For Dummies by Steven Holzner

Radical Forgiveness by Colin C. Tipping

Rich Dad, Poor Dad by Robert T. Kiyosaki

Science of Being in Twenty Seven Lessons by Eugene A. Fersen

Secrets of the Millionaire Mind: Mastering the Inner Game of Wealth by T. Harv Eker

Six Thinking Hats by Edward De Bono

Spiritual Liberation: Fulfilling Your Soul's Potential by Michael Bernard Beckwith

Stillness Speaks by Eckhart Tolle

Strengths Finder 2.0 by Tom Rath

Taking the Quantum Leap: The New Physics for Nonscientists by Fred A. Wolf

The 21 Irrefutable Laws of Leadership by John Maxwell

The Abundance Book by John Randolph Price

The Artist's Way: A Spiritual Path to Higher Creativity by Julia Cameron

The Biology of Belief: Unleashing the Power of Consciousness, Matter & Miracles by Bruce H. Lipton

The Book of Secrets: Unlocking the Hidden Dimensions of Your Life by Deepak Chopra

The Dore Lectures on Mental Science by Thomas Troward

The Field: The Quest for the Secret Force of the Universe by Lynne McTaggart

The Four Spiritual Laws of Prosperity: A Simple Guide to Unlimited Abundance by Edwene Gaines

The Game of Life and How to Play It by Florence Scovel Shinn.

The Goal Achiever by Bob Proctor

The Isaiah Effect: Decoding the Lost Science of Prayer and Prophecy By Gregg Braden

The Law and the Promise by Neville Goddard

The Law and the Word by Thomas Troward

The Law of Attraction: How to Make It Work for You by Esther Hicks, Jerry Hicks

The Law of Divine Compensation: On Work, Money, and Miracles by Marianne Williamson

The Law of Forgiveness: Tap in to the Positive Power of Forgiveness—and Attract Good Things to Your Life by Connie Domino

The Law of Success In Sixteen Lessons by Napoleon Hill

The Light Shall Set You Free by Norma Manalovitch

The Magic of Believing by Claude M. Bristol

The Mind Map Book: How to Use Radiant Thinking to Maximize Your Brain's Untapped Potential by Tony Buzan and Barry Buzan

The Power of Focus: How to Hit your Business, Personal and Financial Targets With Absolute Certainty by Jack Canfield, Mark Victor Hanson and Les Hewitt

The Power of Awareness by Neville Goddard

The Power of Now: A Guide to Spiritual Enlightenment by Eckhart Tolle

The Power of Positive Thinking by Norman Vincent Peale

The Power of Your Subconscious Mind by Joseph Murphy

The Quantum World by Kenneth W. Ford

The Science of Getting Rich by Wallace D. Wattles

The Science of Mind by Ernest Holmes

The Secret by Rhonda Byrne

The Secret Gratitude Book by Rhonda Byrne

The Seven Main Aspects of God by Emmet Fox

The Seven Spiritual Laws of Success by Deepak Chopra

The Strangest Secret by Earl Nightingale

The Success Principles: How to Get from Where You Are to Where You Want to Be by Jack Canfield and Janet Switzer

The Success Puzzle by Bob Proctor

The Wisdom of the Enneagram: The Complete Guide to Psychological and Spiritual Growth for the Nine Personality Types by Russ Hudson and Don Richard Riso

Think and Grow Rich by Napoleon Hill

Three Magic Words by Uell Stanley Anderson

Train Your Mind, Change Your Brain: How a New Science Reveals Our Extraordinary Potential to Transform Ourselves by Sharon Begley

Walking Between the Worlds: The Science of Compassion by Gregg Braden

Wishes Fulfilled: Mastering the Art of Manifesting by Wayne W. Dyer

Working With The Law by Raymond Holliwell

You Can Heal Your Life by Louise Hay

You Were Born Rich: Now You Can Discover And Develop Those Riches by Bob Proctor

You 2: A High Velocity Formula for Multiplying Your Personal Effectiveness in Quantum Leaps by Price Pritchett

Your Faith is Your Fortune by Neville Goddard

Your Greatest Power by J. Martin Kohe

Your Invisible Power by Genevieve Behrend

www.ingramcontent.com/pod-product-compliance
Lightning Source LLC
Chambersburg PA
CBHW070403200326
41518CB00011B/2041